# Praise fo.

MW00618051

"Rosebrock and Henry provide readers with tremendous insight on leadership best practices that move educational institutions from good to great. *Arrows* will undoubtedly steer readers in the right direction as they look to promote the success of all students in an efficient and timely manner. Don't miss out, get your copy today!"

**Brad Currie**, 2017 NASSP National Assistant
Principal of the Year and #Satchat Co-Founder

"This book provides the reader with research-based applications and hands-on ideas that were developed through first-hand experience by the authors. It is a must read to gain best practice instructions, and it will improve the professional development happening in schools and in the business sector. *Arrows* is a pleasure to read, extraordinarily informative, and will help guide future leadership and management decisions."

**Dr. Bret Daghe**, Principal, Brownsburg High School

"This is a guarantee for student learning centered on focus. Aligning arrows in school systems may require bold approaches that will reveal the essential components of learning that have often been lost in band-aids programs that were meant to improve student achievement and instruction."

**Matt Walsh**, Academics Specialist,
Indiana Department of Education

"Highly effective teaching and learning in the K-12 environment today requires a systems approach where educators work collaboratively to deliver high quality curriculum, instruction, and assessment to students. This book effectively outlines how Brownsburg has successfully implemented a systems approach that has benefitted its educators, students, and the community as a whole."

**Dr. Andrew Melin**, Executive Director of the
Central Indiana Educational Service Center

"For years, teachers and leaders have wondered what the secrets behind the success of the highest performing public school district in the state of Indiana are. *Arrows* outlines the district's focus on a narrow and common vision that consistently yields high levels of student achievement and virtually eliminates all achievement gaps. This book is a testament to what a school district can accomplish when all its arrows are pointing in a consistent direction that is focused on equity and high levels of learning for all."

**Tina Seymour**, Author of *Lead From the Start*

# ARROWS

## A Systems-Based Approach
## to School Leadership

Carrie Rosebrock
and Sarah Henry

MIMI & TODD
PRESS

Arrows: A Systems-Based Approach to School Leadership

For information about this title or to order other books and/or electronic media, contact the publisher:

Mimi &Todd Press
4629 Cass Street, #292
San Diego, CA 92109
www.mimitoddpress.com

ISBN:     978-1-950089-06-2 (paperback)
          978-1-950089-07-9 (ebook)

Printed in the United States of America

Publisher: Starr Sackstein
Program Director: Paul Bloomberg
Publishing Manager: Tony Francoeur
Production Editor: Starr Sackstein
Copy Editor: Terri Lee Paulsen
Book Designer/Typesetter: Van-Garde Imagery, Inc.
Indexer: Alison Cox
Cover Designer: Paul Hamilton, III
Art Director: Alison Cox
Marketing Manager: Donnie Luehring
Office Manager: Leah Tierney

# Dedication

This book is dedicated to the educational leaders
who continue to search for and create equitable
learning experiences for all.

# Acknowledgments

To our students and families of Brownsburg Community School Corporation: It is because of you and your desire to create a community centered on high-quality learning opportunities for all that this book is even possible. We have both spent the majority of our careers teaching and learning with you, and we are grateful for this experience. You value open, honest dialogue and expect the very best from your schools. To our students in particular, thank you for the joy, laughter, connection, and education you have given us, and for what you've taught us about dignity and belonging.

To our teachers and staff: Biased as this may be, we believe many of the best teachers in the country live and work in Brownsburg, Indiana. You confront challenges with grace and determination. You work to create safe learning spaces for all students. You push each other to grow and refine your craft. You are the most talented, dedicated, open-hearted, passionate individuals we know. From working beside you in classrooms, teams, and buildings, to trusting your abilities to teach our own children, we are forever grateful to the teaching and learning staff in Brownsburg. We often say here that it's about People, Not Programs—and you, our teachers, are our people.

To the PLC leaders in Brownsburg Community School Corporation: You are amazing. You are relentless. You are team builders, agenda creators, note revisors, and student advocates. It is not easy leading teams of peers, but it is because of your ability to create collaborative, focused teams that Brownsburg students have experienced the high-quality learning environments that exist today. You are also the reason the learning will always continue to improve.

To our leadership team: It has been one of the privileges of our respective careers to be leaders alongside such tremendous educators in Brownsburg. No superintendent can lead a district by themselves, and we are grateful for the tremendous support, camaraderie, and collaboration among the district-level leadership team. You are the reason the arrows align at all levels. Thank you for the hard conversations, for your willingness to sit in discomfort for the betterment of students and the team, for creating a culture that is more about the team than the individual, and for pushing us to think differently about learning.

To Dr. Jim Snapp, superintendent of Brownsburg Community School Corporation: Leadership begins at the top, and we thank you for always being willing to lead. It is because of your vision that our educational community, together, was able to leap from good to great. You planted the seeds of this book throughout the years by creating a culture grounded in growth, learning, and relationships. Thank you for making the tough calls when they need to be made and for continually reflecting on how we can all get better. Thank you for trusting us to tell the story.

To Dr. Kat Jessup, assistant superintendent of Brownsburg Community School Corporation: Thank you for giving us room to grow, lead, create, hire, coach, and connect. You instill a sense of trust and respect for the leaders you coach, and we appreciate your ability and willingness to ask the right questions at the right time. Thank you for always starting a meeting by asking about our families and for knowing how to win over a group with honesty, humor, and humility. You are one of the strongest instructional leaders we know, and we are honored to have been able to grow and learn with you.

To Dr. Bret Daghe, principal of Brownsburg High School: To begin, we would like to thank you for guiding us as we transitioned into secondary leadership roles. Despite us having only middle school experience, you trusted us to learn the ins and outs of a high school, and you frequently empowered us to lead and grow. You modeled for us what it means to be a servant leader, how to care about our people, and how to embrace others' unique traits and skills. You are a leader who has listened, encouraged, and celebrated the success of your team. Thank you for giving us the room and space to grow. You are more than a leader and mentor to us; you are our friend.

To our fellow secondary department heads: Thank you for being a strong support network day in and day out. You've shaped who we are as instructional leaders, and we have loved growing alongside you. We often say that coaching and leading teachers and other leaders is a tremendous honor and gift, but it is also uniquely challenging as we try to create a balance among multiple buildings. Thank you for dressing up on spirit days, for laughing until we cry in meetings, for dealing with our idiosyncrasies, and for allowing us to be vulnerable. You are true teammates.

To RICK DOSS, DIRECTOR OF Secondary Education, MSD Washington Township: Thank you for seeing the potential in each of us and for being the principal who brought us into Brownsburg. You are a guiding leadership voice for many around the state of Indiana. You are also the reason we connected, as you put us on a team together that started our professional and personal relationships.

To AMBER SCHROERING AND BRAD Currie: Thank you for encouraging, connecting, and promoting our work. When we were seeking a publisher for the manuscript, we asked our good friend Amber if she had any ideas of who we might reach out to. The one name she shared was her good friend Brad Currie, and Brad in turn shared our work with our publisher, Starr Sackstein. Amber and Brad, you connected us to exactly where we needed to be, and you truly represent the collaborative spirit of educators in our field. You are both phenomenal leaders.

To MATT WALSH AND SARA Reeves: Thank you for helping the two of us remember to laugh and enjoy the job, even on the toughest of days. Your dance moves and stapling abilities are top-notch in our book. Thank you for keeping our connection strong regardless of our evolving roles and experiences.

To OUR PUBLISHING TEAM AT Mimi & Todd Press: Thank you for jumping into this project with the two of us. We are honored to represent Mimi & Todd and everything your community represents. Thank you to Starr Sackstein, our publisher, who has coached and guided our work. Thank you to the artistic team of Alison Cox and Paul Hamilton for your brilliant work on the cover and layout. Thank you to our copy editor, Terri Lee Paulsen, for reviewing the manuscript with a fine-tooth comb.

To OUR FRIENDS AND FAMILIES: Thank you, Erik, Jenna, Brennan, Brad, Grace, and Will. Without the love, encouragement, and support from our families, this book would not have become a reality. You believe in us and show us love every day. And, finally, thank you to all of our friends who have encouraged us throughout this journey--to believe in ourselves that we could write and publish this book.

# Table of Contents

# Foreword

SYSTEMS THINKING IS A TERM some would argue as cold, personally detached, and disconnected from the true purpose of education. Starting a conversation with the goal of putting a system in place most certainly guarantees frustration, eye rolls, and the hope that this too shall pass. So why even engage in conversation about systems? Simply put: systems work. Students achieve at higher levels and educators are more effective while feeling a greater sense of accomplishment and satisfaction as professionals in well-designed systems.

So, if you can convince lead educators that systems really do work—students achieve more and educators experience the highest levels of satisfaction in their careers, then why aren't more people fully embracing putting educational systems in place? Complexity. Systems are infinitely complex. Even the most accomplished educator can spend an entire career and never figure out all the interconnectedness of the most effective systems. The other significant roadblock is the shift to doing far less in many areas of our professional lives. This includes the abandonment of ineffective practices and the outright refusal to take on new tasks and responsibilities without strong justification. These reasons alone are most often enough for even the most dedicated educators to reexamine the status quo and determine, with a few tweaks, the path they are on is good enough.

Let's be clear, *Arrows* will leave you with more questions than you had prior to reading the book, but these will be deeper, more impactful questions than previously imagined. Yet even as the authors lay out the details of this important work, it will generate additional questions about how to do this work in your school or district. This work is not for the fainthearted. This work is for educators who have grown frustrated with disconnected professional development, curriculum work, and school improvement efforts that do nothing but consume time. For many who have devoted countless hours to initiative after initiative only to be met with something new, there is hope. I only ask that you read this critical work about how committed educators with a vision of how it could be better made the decision to dramatically change course. This transformational approach led to greater results for their students and the highest levels of professional fulfillment.

While I did not write *Arrows*, I am very proud of it. The authors were part of the initial group of lead educators at the start of this work. They provided insights from the early stages of implementing systems. Their viewpoints reflect a frontline perspective of how best to navigate potential pitfalls, have critical conversations, and fully understand the importance of "the Burden of No"—saying no to disconnected initiatives and work that does not fit the system.

You will see me personally referenced in the text of this book, and while it is most certainly flattering, please don't be fooled. This transformation of an entire school district is the amalgamation of the thoughts, actions, and leadership of the most committed educators with whom I have ever been associated in nearly four decades of public education.

My greatest hope for you is that this book sparks an understanding that our schools can be better, regardless of how good they are right now, and it equips you with the knowledge to begin this critically important work. Students can achieve more—without sacrificing those essential student–teacher relationships that drew us to the profession in the first place. Collegial relationships will be deepened to a level not previously achieved. *Arrows* is a call to focus on the essential practices that work, capitalizing on the power of connecting those practices in a system that is logical and most certainly more effective than any other strategy currently in place in our schools.

**Dr. Jim Snapp**, Superintendent of Brownsburg
Community School Corporation

# Introduction

## What Would Happen?

THIS IS THE ESSENTIAL QUESTION we are attempting to answer throughout this book. Learning in the United States has become increasingly polarized, monetized, and politicized. Innovations and technologies often muddle our understanding of so-called best practices and strategies for learning. In many communities, students and families are afforded more choices in school selection than ever before in the history of American education. Schools, even within singular communities, often find themselves pitted against one another in an attempt to woo or outshine their neighbors. There is a pervasive, creeping idea that has burrowed its way into the psyche of many American parents, students, and even teachers: schools are failing.

But what would happen if the competitive edge—if the question for innovation—was muted? What would happen if a district, not merely a singular school, decided to take the bold step to put into practice much of what modern educational research claims to authentically impact student learning? If a common, viable curriculum was adopted by all teachers, in all disciplines and age groups? If quality common assessments were the expectation, not the exception? If professional learning communities—a buzz phrase in recent years that has morphed into its own quasi-synonym for anything from data meeting to "self-care hour"—remained student centered, focused, and implemented with fidelity? What if we actually trained and coached our teachers all throughout their careers so that stagnation never set in? What if we equipped our staff with the tools needed to read data and respond in real time with interventions and enrichment?

What if we took a step back from technology, the one-to-one craze, and asked ourselves if a screen can really replicate the engagement of learning created between a highly effective teacher and a group of students? What if we didn't follow the trends? What if, instead, we reset them?

What if, instead of leaning into trends and programs, we chose to lean into people? To unpack what it means to create a dignified space for all students, teachers, and leaders in our schools? What if we chose to create a new system, one of dignity and belonging, where *all* students' learning needs were met, embraced, and celebrated? What if there was a way to create a focused, student-centered vision for learning in our schools?

## Arrows

Every summer, we host a new-teacher breakfast for incoming staff across our district. Our superintendent welcomes new teachers and leads a presentation that looks remarkably similar, year after year. His message stays on point for a reason; he calls this "**purposeful redundancy**," and we'll reference this phrase (and many others) throughout the book. One of Dr. Snapp's points of emphasis each year is to explain that in our school system, we believe in "**people, not programs.**" As heads around the room begin to nod, he explains that far too often school leaders are tempted to distract their teachers by asking them to focus on too many competing ideas—too many arrows. From committees, to professional development, from fundraisers to curricular approaches, there is too much going on, in all directions, for clarity to impact teachers.

When there are too many arrows, heading in all directions, teachers and staff are left with a sense of overwhelm and confusion about the vision of their school.

## Compare the Two Approaches

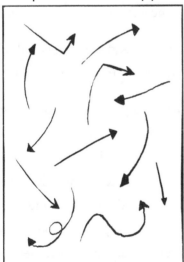 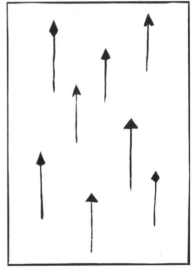

**Figure I.1:** This simple image describes programmatic approaches in schools across the United States. Compare to Figure I.2, which illustrates how a district can create a clear vision.

**Figure I. 2:** Streamlined Approach to School Leadership

Figures I.2 is a perfect examples of how school leaders should imagine their vision unfolding in real life. Teachers and staff want to follow clear paths. They want to know what exactly is expected of them, and they want to please so that students can benefit from that clarity of vision and focus.

Too many arrows create varied interpretations of expectations—for staff and students alike.

But here's the beauty behind this issue: you have the power, control, and influence to not only align the arrows in your school but to eliminate some as well.

This book is our bold challenge to each and every leader in education today. Cut the fluff. Stop the onslaught of initiatives (year after year after year). Simplify the execution of your vision.

Imagine the impact on student outcomes and achievements if the arrows were all heading in the same direction—to the same target.

We wrote *Arrows* as a guide to help you get from simply imagining the impact to the reality of seeing the results of systems and clarity up close. We're excited that our district has experienced the tremendous development and success that it has over these past 10 years, but that's not enough. We need you and your teachers and your students to experience this growth, too. We're in the field of best is good, but better is best—and we're here to help you and your district get even better.

**People, not programs.**

**Similar to identical.**

**Tight-Loose-Tight.**

**J-curve.**

**The Burden of No.**

**Purposeful redundancy.**

These are all catchphrases and mantras that we believe help to simplify the focus and help align the arrows.

You probably have your own catchphrases and sayings that describe the focus of your district. Perhaps some of your sayings actually illustrate just how cluttered and confusing your district's vision is—if you believe your district operates with a vision to begin with.

Do your teachers know the vision—these mantras? Do they repeat them to friends who ask about their corporation or school? Do they excitedly describe the PLC process that they experience or the support they receive from their administrators and coaches? Are they happy? How do you know?

Do students return to your high school just to thank their teachers for preparing and caring about them as much as they did? Do former graduates stop you in Walmart to share they're transferring schools because the esteemed university they chose wasn't as organized as their high school and they couldn't justify wasting money on a school that didn't know who they were? How many former graduates have returned to teach in your schools? Do you know?

## How to Read This Book

*Arrows* is the story of a district that went from good to great seemingly overnight. It is written from the shared perspective of two teachers turned curriculum administrators who were a part of the transformation process (and after).

We are teacher leaders at heart, and we wrote this book to share the story of our schools so that other leaders, specifically principals and central office leaders, can hear insider perspectives on the power of clarity. We wrote this book to share the steps to take to create a curriculum-rich, instructionally sound, and *happy* district staff who impacts the lives of their students each and every day.

We know our district is not your district, but there are nuggets here—golden pieces of hard-fought lessons—and we ask that you read with ears, eyes, and hearts wide open.

We are tired of people asking questions and not having the answers. For years, our district leadership team would joke about, "One day, when we write the book ..." and then about a year ago, the two of us sat down and said, "One day is now. Let's do it—let's get this information *out there*."

So we did. We tell much of *Arrows* from our first-person perspective, and we don't hold back. Carrie's voice is the first-person account used to narrate the book, as we wanted to create a simple reading experience for our audience. This book isn't riddled with light suggestions; it's not our hope that you pick and choose a few ideas that sound like they may work for *your* staff and *your* students.

We wrote *Arrows* because we have seen and felt the incredible impact that clarity and expectations have on *learning*, and we're tired of educators (namely leaders) mucking this up.

*Arrows* is our attempt to provide school leaders everywhere the clarity that truly changes everything about how we approach equitable learning for students and teachers.

If you're tired of the spinning plates, tired of convincing your teachers that this really *is* the last initiative, tired of blaming the state for the test scores, tired of feeling like you're running a race you cannot win, then this book is for you.

We give you permission to stop trying to do it all, and we invite you to lead your district in a new direction.

We promise you won't get lost.

**Just follow the arrows.**

Chapter 1:

# The Brownsburg Way

"Excellence is to do a common thing
in an uncommon way."

– Booker T. Washington

## Welcome to Brownsburg, Home of the Bulldogs

THE FIRST THING I NOTICED was the purple street signs with their little bulldog logos. It was June 2006, and I had an interview at Brownsburg East Middle School in the morning. My dad wanted to drive me to the little westside suburb outside of Indianapolis to make sure I knew where I was going. Before I even met my future principal, I was smitten. This town clearly cared about its schools, and I desperately wanted them to care about me.

The town itself is nothing to gawk at. When driving in from Indianapolis, there is a short lull between it and its famous neighbor, Speedway (home of the Indianapolis 500). Dotted with corn fields, houses, and another tiny town, the entrance into Brownsburg is less than glamorous. In many respects, Brownsburg looks like many other small towns or suburbs around the United States. There are small businesses in strip malls built in the 1970s. There are empty grocery store buildings that are now up for lease. There's the best little donut shop in town, several gas stations, and your pick of fast-food options. Brownsburg is largely a residential town, with a population of 24,072. The median income for households is $69,647, and the median home value is $153,000. The bulk of its tax base comes from residential, not business. Its largest employer is the school corporation, with Walmart and O'Reilly Auto Parts coming in second and third, respectively.

There's a reason visitors notice those purple street signs at first glance. The heart of this community is found in its schools. In 2018, Brownsburg Community School Corporation had 9,296 students enrolled in its PreK–12 courses. It opened its seventh elementary school, which would feed into one of its two middle schools. It was also amid a massive renovation project to its one high school—built in the early 1970s and situated smack-dab in the middle of town. In fact, all of Brownsburg's schools are found in the middle of the town. Brownsburg describes its setup as a campus feel, meaning each of the 13 schools are within an approximate 1-mile radius of each other. The proximity of the schools to one another, as well as their physical positions in the town, reiterate at the most obvious and basic level that the schools truly are the center of this universe.

## Growth

Brownsburg wasn't always the burgeoning school system that it is today. In the 2005–2006 school year, Brownsburg Community School District had 6,726 students enrolled in its schools. There were five elementary schools, one middle school, and a high school that housed about 1,400 students. It was inconspicuous, the way most middle-class suburbs are. National Pee-Wee Baseball Champs signs welcomed you into town, along with a list of nearly 30 faith-based organizations. It was quiet, and most definitely off the radar.

The schools themselves were relatively solid. This was before the onslaught of standardized testing, school takeovers, and letter grades. The graduation rate for the class of 2009 was 91%, yet the high school was considered to be on Academic Watch according to the state. In 2009, 80.8% of the students in grades 3–8 passed the English standardized assessment while 84.7% passed math.

Table 1.1

| 2009 Data Snapshot | | |
|---|---|---|
| Graduation Rate | ELA ISTEP | Math ISTEP |
| 91% | 80.8% | 84.7% |

If you go back further in Brownsburg's history, you will see a steady trend of how this middle-working-class town slowly grew from a predominantly farming community in the 1950s to its quintessential suburban status of the present. Again, there is nothing flashy about this community. Most of the homes were built between 1940 and 1980. Recent years have brought about a major renovation to the "downtown" area in an attempt to modernize and attract younger professionals to move here. A few parks dot the landscape, but so do empty parking lots. For all intents and purposes, there is nothing special about the physicality of this town that has drawn families to move to the Westside in droves since 2010.

Unless, of course, you consider the current status of the schools.

## A District Approach

Since 2011, the Brownsburg Community School Corporation has been an established and bona fide powerhouse. Over the past two years, I've heard other district leaders refer to Brownsburg as a "juggernaut," "the gold standard," and simply, "the best." At the time that this book is being written, all nine eligible schools have earned four stars from the state of Indiana (the highest possible rating) along with A letter grades (the highest possible rating) for the past four years in a row. They are the only school system in the state to do so with each of its schools. More? They have also accumulated four Blue Ribbon School designations in as many years, and have performed at the top—the very top—on state assessments in math, language arts, and students passing both.

Why is this impressive—these stars and letter grades and ribbons and numbers? Because we are talking about the entire *district*. Not one school this year but not the next. Not this middle school but not that one. Not this side of town but not that side of town. Brownsburg's story is about how an entire district of 13 schools works together to care about the needs of all of its students in the community.

What do you typically see in districts if not this? A handful of schools thrive while others do not. Or, a school performs well one year but not the next. There is no consistency; there is competition; and there are far too many arrows.

So, what exactly did we do?

In 2010, Brownsburg ranked 18th overall with students passing both the English and math portions of the Indiana Statewide Testing for Educational Progress, or ISTEP. In 2012, we jumped to 5th; in 2013, we were 3rd, and since 2016, we have been ranked the number 1 school system in the state for the past five years in a row. A table with this data can be found on A1 of the Appendix.

## A1: Longitudinal State Assessment Data

| Brownsburg Community School Corporation-Trend Data | | | | | | | |
|---|---|---|---|---|---|---|---|
| ELA | | Math | | Both ELA & Math | | Official State Rank | |
| Year | District Passing % | Year | District Passing % | Year | District Passing % | Year | Rank |
| 1996 | 77.1 | 1996 | 77.1 | 1996 | | 1996 | |
| 1997 | 81.5 | 1997 | 78.2 | 1997 | | 1997 | |
| 1998 | 83.2 | 1998 | 80.1 | 1998 | | 1998 | |
| 1999 | 79.5 | 1999 | 81.1 | 1999 | | 1999 | |
| 2000 | 80.8 | 2000 | 84.7 | 2000 | | 2000 | |
| 2001 | 80.0 | 2001 | 83.5 | 2001 | | 2001 | |
| 2002 | 81.8 | 2002 | 82.7 | 2002 | | 2002 | |
| 2003 | 83.4 | 2003 | 84.3 | 2003 | | 2003 | |
| 2004 | 83.8 | 2004 | 85.2 | 2004 | | 2004 | |
| 2005 | 82.7 | 2005 | 86.0 | 2005 | 78.0 | 2005 | 21 |
| 2006 | 83.1 | 2006 | 85.7 | 2006 | 78.4 | 2006 | 22 |
| 2007 | 83.1 | 2007 | 84.7 | 2007 | 77.6 | 2007 | 23 |
| 2008F | 81.5 | 2008F | 83.6 | 2008F | 75.8 | 2008F | 31 |
| 2009S | 82.3 | 2009S | 82.3 | 2009S | 76.4 | 2009S | 21 |
| 2010S | 85.3 | 2010S | 88.1 | 2010S | 81.1 | 2010S | 18 |
| 2011 | 86.9 | 2011 | 90.4 | 2011 | 84.9 | 2011 | 17 |
| 2012 | 90.0 | 2012 | 93.2 | 2012 | 88.3 | 2012 | 5 |
| 2013 | 91.4 | 2013 | 94.8 | 2013 | 89.4 | 2013 | 5 |
| 2014 | 91.8 | 2014 | 95.9 | 2014 | 90.5 | 2014 | 6 |
| 2015* | 85.6% | 2015 | 86.4% | 2015 | 79.7% | 2015 | 3 |
| 2016** | 87.2% | 2016 | 88.0% | 2016 | 82.1% | 2016 | 1 |
| 2017** | 88.3% | 2017 | 88.0% | 2017 | 83.1% | 2017 | 1 |
| 2018** | 88.5% | 2018 | 89.2% | 2018 | 83.6% | 2018 | 1 |
| *2015 ISTEP+ recut to CCR standards | | | | | | | |
| **2016 ISTEP+ does not include grade 10 | | | | | | | |

Brownsburg High School, which had been on Academic Watch in 2010 has been an A school since the 2015–2016 school year, with graduation rates averaging between 96% and 99% each year, with a rate of 99.1% in 2019.

We never set out to be number one. That was never the goal. But for the past 11 years, the district goal has been simple and clear: implement PLCs with fidelity, narrow achievement gaps, and improve our results. The focus was on student achievement and collective growth. To accomplish these goals, we relentlessly clarify expectations and eliminate arrows as often as possible.

There is no question about the success of the schools as measured by state assessments, graduation rates, AP scores, or consistent attendance. What should be questioned is how it is even possible for not one school but all 13 to achieve the highest ratings possible all while poverty rates increased equally across the district. Between 2011 and 2020, poverty rates in our community rose from about 16% to nearly 30%. Student enrollment increased, funding turned stagnant (in fact, we are one of the few districts to have a failed referendum) but still, achievement rose. How is this possible?

A typically high-performing school is just that—a school on its own. Perhaps a few other schools in its district will shine a little brighter than the rest, but overall, books in education are usually based on studies completed on individual schools, not whole districts. To fully understand how and why Brownsburg has become what it is—an exemplary model for how to systematically increase student achievement for all students—you must look at its story differently. In Brownsburg, it's about *all* of the schools' mission to work together to achieve greater results.

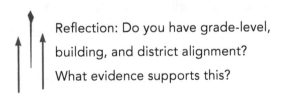

Reflection: Do you have grade-level, building, and district alignment? What evidence supports this?

## Higher Achievement, Together

A common and necessary starting point in all organizations is to simplify your vision and mission so that everyone involved in the company can fulfill said visions to the best of their abilities at all times. In Brownsburg, the vision is simple: *Higher Achievement, Together.* This vision has not changed in over a decade, but 11 years ago the execution of this vision received a major facelift.

*Higher Achievement, Together* is the mantra that drives all decisions made from the top (superintendent) all the way to the roots of classified employees. Brownsburg's vision keeps one main focus a priority above all others: students enter the doors of their schools to learn and to achieve their highest potentials as learners. In subsequent chapters of this book, we will draw the map in great detail as to how this higher achievement is accomplished, but the core essence of each school in this system is that students are there to learn. Doesn't seem too hard, right? After all, we are talking about an educational system.

The second part of this guiding vision is *Together.* There is a tangible belief among all staff in the Brownsburg Community School Corporation that all students deserve the opportunities to learn in equitable environments. No one elementary is better than another. No one school is stacked with higher poverty rates than the others. In all decisions for students, the goal is equity and a sense of communal, systemic approaches to concerns.

We can't tell you how many times school teams have visited to observe our systems—whether for elementary, secondary, special education, or PLCs. Visiting teachers are quick to ask questions and quick to share; one of the most commonly shared reflections is that some schools in their districts seem to "have it together" while others do not. We totally understand the natural tendency for self-preservation via comparison, but unfortunately, this type of toxic finger-pointing is eating districts alive—and they don't even know it!

The last thing a school district wants is to have the perception that one school, or several, make the "it" list while others get left behind. In fact, this is a continual battle that leadership chooses to fight within this district to protect the system. Uncomfortable conversations occur if one elementary school does a book study and the rest do not. With two middle schools, there is seemingly constant discussion about how both schools are viewed within the community and how both schools are working to collaborate as one. At the end of the day, it is the district's vision, not each individual school's, that anchors decisions.

From a staff perspective, *Together* is the glue that holds these systems in place. There is a consistent expectation that the leaders at the highest levels are working in open communication to make decisions as a team. What does open communication mean? Real, honest, often difficult and uncomfortable conversations must be had. Feelings may get hurt. Egos are set aside. Leaders are asked to share their personal goals with one another and then to hold each other accountable when they fall short.

It is difficult to be honest 100% of the time—and still maintain rapport, collegiality, and trust. To have these kinds of tough leadership conversations, leaders must buy-in to the idea that feedback of all kinds is needed, beneficial, and ultimately how they choose to operate. This is still something we struggle with as a district.

There are checks and balances among various leaders in the district; there are goal statements and leadership retreats. There are 360 feedback processes and staff surveys administered. This belief that "we are better together" permeates all decisions and is the foundational basis for the district's professional development beliefs as well. This district does not believe in programs, but rather its people; therefore, teachers meet in weekly team meetings—**professional learning communities** (or PLCs). It is through this expected constant collaboration among teachers that they and their leaders are able to ensure the equity in both curriculum and instruction for all students. The PLC process is described in detail in Chapter 5, and it is the vital lifeline supporting staff and student growth.

Different schools and leaders refer to PLCs by various titles. Some call them grade-level meetings, department meetings, or teams. Authors Paul Bloomberg and Barb Pitchford refer to PLCs as Impact Teams and describe them as teams that "meet for the express purpose of learning together in service to all students."

Most schools and organizations believe that they have clear vision and mission statements, but the reality is that most members of these groups have no clue what they are. How can an individual, let alone a group, fulfill a mission if they have no idea what it is to begin with? The unsettling truth is that today's educational landscape contains far too many teachers and staff members unsure of their own school's target goals.

When I (Carrie) was working on my master's in administration, one of our assignments was to review our school's improvement plan and bring it to class for peer critique. While the other 19 members of my cohort nodded easily and jotted down this task on their to-do lists, I began to panic. I had no idea what our school improvement plan was or where to find it. I asked for clarification (and sounded like a real dope) when I said, "Do all schools have an SIP? Because I don't think Brownsburg does." I was assured that we did, in fact have one—and that if I asked my principal, she'd point me to it.

My mind started to reel. Typically in my admin classes, I left feeling proud and assured of the direction of my district. Usually, topics we studied in class were already happening full-throttle in my district. I also boasted about the clarity of our leadership and our collective efficacy. So, how in the world, I wondered, could I not know our SIP?

I decided to meet with our superintendent, Dr. Snapp, and ask him my questions. Remember, I was a classroom teacher at this point, just starting my admin program. We scheduled a meeting the same day that I sent my email, and by the end of the week he came to visit me during prep. He brought along with him an eight-page document, "Brownsburg Community School Corporation's School Improvement Plan," and handed it to me.

I quickly scanned the document, sighed with relief that we did in fact have one, and started to ask my questions.

"Dr. Snapp—why didn't I know about this? Shouldn't I know about this? Do other teachers or buildings know and we did something wrong?"

He kind of chuckled and began to explain. "The state requires that every school has a school improvement plan, regardless of achievement, growth, or results. What used to happen in our district is what happens in nearly all districts and schools still. Each school would have a team of teachers who were on the school improvement plan committee. This committee would meet biweekly to review and write the school's plan. Nearly all of the time was spent writing it and little time was left to implement it. Most plans would become monsters—totaling anywhere between 70 and 100 pages long. When the plan was done, it would be sent to the state, put in a binder, and forgotten. No one knew—especially not the teachers outside of the committee—what the plan was."

I nodded. This made sense. He kept going.

"So, if you think back to when I first started, there were all of these committees, all of these programs that teachers were attempting to implement. Too many arrows, going every which way. We realized that each school essentially needed to have a short, manageable number of goals, and we wanted each school's goals to be similar to identical. Rather than ask teachers to spend hours upon hours writing and revising these huge documents, we have our **data and testing coordinator** for the district write and revise each school's draft. Principals are able to review the drafts, suggest edits, and then we send them in. All that typically changes from school to school are the exact numbers, which are based on the previous year's data. Otherwise, they are exactly the same."

Clarity. Similar to identical. Arrows.

I got it all.

"So, you can find our SIP on the district site if you do some digging, but our teachers don't need to see this document. Carrie, what are your school's goals?" he questioned.

"Implement PLCs with fidelity; achieve a 90% or higher pass rate on ISTEP for math and achieve a 90% or higher pass rate for ELA," I replied.

"Exactly," Dr. Snapp agreed. "You don't need to see this document to know what you're working on. We're doing our due diligence to make our goals as clear as possible so that teachers can know just that easily what their targets are. You see, you knew the school improvement plan—it's the district's plan—and it's those three goals. That's it."

Reflecting back on this conversation some nine years later, I think it's safe to say that both Dr. Snapp and I felt a bit of relief. I felt assured once more that my district was actually as aligned as I'd been imagining—and I'd say he felt the same way. The purpose behind streamlining the SIP process had been accomplished: teachers knew the goals and were busy pursuing them (instead of writing them).

This is just one of many examples of how districts can purposefully take steps to clarify the vision and eliminate unnecessary arrows.

Often teachers have no clue what it is they are working toward as a school, let alone a corporation, and many teachers are operating in survival mode each and every day. Rather than driving toward their school vision, they are creating their own sets of expectations for high achievement—entirely dependent on the preferences of staff and students in the class. When a school, and we will argue a district, is devoid of a clear vision and mission, learning targets are veiled and, therefore, impossible to hit. Because how can you hit a moving target that you didn't even know existed?

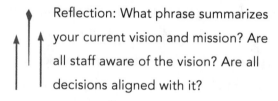

Reflection: What phrase summarizes your current vision and mission? Are all staff aware of the vision? Are all decisions aligned with it?

## Setting the Target

Let's go back just a little further to explain how this vision began in the first place. In 2010, the Brownsburg school board had a decision to make. Their superintendent of the past 15 years was about to retire, and the assistant superintendent was not interested in the position. Along with several other viable candidates, a Brownsburg High School graduate, Jim Snapp, decided to enter his name into the hat.

Dr. Snapp had experience as a social studies teacher, middle school principal, curriculum director, assistant superintendent, and adjunct professor at the University of Indianapolis. Though he had been a bulldog all of his life, he was in fact the board's second choice for the position. But when the top candidate bowed out of the race, Dr. Snapp was offered the position of his lifetime—to be superintendent of his home town.

## Year One

To better understand the state of the union, Dr. Snapp spent the duration of his first year as superintendent doing what most new leaders should do: he listened. He met with hundreds of teachers and staff to hear their opinions of what was going right—and often, what was going wrong—in the district. He asked a few questions, nodded along to the insights shared, and took notes.

Many of his teacher meetings were conducted over his first summer, and I was one of the teachers from our building who went to meet with him.

Dr. Snapp is a tall, cheerful man of solid stature. He's quick to reach for your hand and introduce himself as Jim, and that's precisely what he did at our first meeting. From the start, I felt like he was ready to lead—perhaps because mostly what he did was listen. We sat down, he explained that he wanted to take 20 minutes of my time, and asked me to share what I thought about the district, initiatives, curriculum, and so on.

I was one of the many teachers that summer who explained that we felt we had too many spinning plates. We knew we had good schools, but we lacked direction. I shared that we admired our leaders, but they didn't always seem to work together across buildings. Jim (as he prefers to be called) asked a few questions here and there, but mostly he sat and jotted down notes. He wanted to know about me, my teaching career thus far, my family, and what I loved about our district. It was a short, meaningful conversation, and when the 20 minutes were up, true to his word, we wrapped.

Teachers want leaders with vision who can listen and lead at the same time. We want to know our voices are heard—but that at the end of the day, someone will make the tough decisions. Even from our first interaction, I could tell that Jim intended to lead with intention and clarity—even if at times this caused discomfort.

I wasn't alone in my feedback that day. Teachers consistently shared a deep connection and pride they felt in their schools. They felt valued by their building leaders; parent support was strong; morale was a solid B. On the surface, Brownsburg was absolutely a great school system to work in. Compared to other neighboring schools, it stacked right up. Class sizes were average, competition of wages was present, and teachers felt a freedom to make decisions in their classrooms.

But this is where the feedback shifts.

Across the corporation, teachers and staff felt as if a potpourri of programs were implemented with inefficiency on a yearly basis. Leaders and teachers might attend various national and local conferences. After, the lucky attendees were responsible for presenting the entire conference in one 45-minute staff meeting—essentially for their peers to use or lose. One school might focus on a PD thread that another school had never heard of.

Professional development was a dreaded experience because all too often outside presenters were sharing the next flavor of the month initiative only to abandon it before the end of the year.

This glut of programs, professional development, and initiatives is reflective of many schools across our nation's landscape. Brownsburg was not unique in any way. There were committees for various school-wide programs, and teachers were required to join one or two of these committees each year. Staple committees included topics like bullying prevention, school improvement planning, and cultural competency. Each of these focus areas—on the surface—appears to be an absolutely needed element of every school across this country. And because of this appearance, nearly all schools across this country do in fact have these committees.

Many of our schools also had **RTI** (Response to Intervention), student activities, social chairs, and faculty meeting planning committees. Teachers met in their respective committees perhaps once a month for anywhere from 45 to 60 minutes. Some committees carried over from year to year; some did not. The creation of committees, as well as their effectiveness, was left entirely to school principals.

In addition to the long list of initiatives, curriculum development was entirely in the hands of each individual teacher. There was no expectation that teachers implement a common curriculum, nor were they required to give common assessments. If a set of triplets attended Brown Elementary School and each was in their own class separate from their siblings, there was no guarantee that these students within the same family were having an equitable learning experience. Jill's teacher might decide to have her write for 60 minutes a day where Josie's might only have her write for 10.

When we view curriculum from the perspective of the parents of these triplets, obvious concerns begin to surface. Who would be okay with one daughter receiving 600% more instruction in writing than another?

Apply this same open concept of curriculum to higher-level courses—courses that determine students' GPA—and a different concern about equity arises. Brownsburg High School did not require its teachers to use common grading practices—even within the same course—so there was no real way of measuring the authenticity of what those grades represented beyond each individual teacher's classroom. An A in Mrs. Johnson's class might earn you a C+ in Mr. Beck's class—and there was no real way of knowing. Did Mrs. Johnson and Mr. Beck have the professional freedom to determine learning practices that best suited their teaching styles? Absolutely! Was there any way to assess whether their teaching styles made positive or negative impacts on student learning? Absolutely not.

Here's the harsh reality: there has been a pervasive belief among many teachers in the United States that their classroom is their castle and they alone should determine what occurs inside the walls. Unfortunately, when given the freedom to create individualized curriculum, teachers, schools, and districts are creating a cauldron of learning experiences that all too often negatively impact students. A teacher's sense of autonomy should not come at the expense of a student's ability to grow and thrive.

With clear feedback from his teachers, and a career's worth of educational research and best practice regarding leadership,

Dr. Snapp made a bold move. He concluded that in order to best meet the needs of his students he would need to narrow the focus within the district to strictly focus on a common vision. Where many leaders have the intent of creating clarity but often fail, Brownsburg chose a system that would ensure the vision remained clear and all students were offered the very best learning experiences possible.

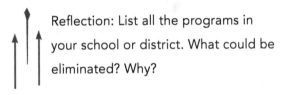

Reflection: List all the programs in your school or district. What could be eliminated? Why?

# Chapter 2:
# Similar to Identical

"One of the most significant factors that
impacts student achievement is that teachers
commit to implementing a common and
viable curriculum to ensure no matter who
teaches a given class, the curriculum will
address certain essential content."

– Robert Marzano

READY FOR A BIG, BOLD claim: if public education is to become
the great equalizer for children in all social classes, then there is
no more important concept for school leaders than the belief in
the phrase "Similar to Identical."

You might ask: Similar to what? Identical to whom? How many
varying shades of similarities are needed before two fill-in-the-blank
anything become one? Do we really *want* everything to be the same?
What about differentiation? What about creative expression? What
about the prerogative of the empowered leaders who have been hired
to guide their classes, schools, and districts? Don't their individual
voices have any authority in decision-making anymore?

You wouldn't be alone, but you also wouldn't be correct.

## A Working Definition

Similar to identical is a belief that two or more aspects (i.e., curriculum, assessments, teacher evaluations, faculty meetings, processes across buildings) are monitored inside of a system that promotes commonalities over individualism. To be similar to identical is to adhere to a collective drive to make decisions in groups and then follow through with the expectations that are set.

This way of approaching education (or any organization for that matter) needs to include:

1. **Equity**
2. **Systems**
3. **Alignment**
4. **Goals**

For two or more things to be similar to identical, there must be systems in place that create the clarity of expectations for all involved. Without a clear system of expectations and protocols, even the best people will fail.

In my current role as a learning specialist who works with teachers and leaders across our state, the lack of similar-to-identical expectations throughout districts is the top complaint, concern, and constriction shared by teachers. As teachers share the lack of vision and accountability in their districts, I nod and empathize, but internally I'm screaming. I want so desperately to call their principals and superintendents and say, "Here is what they need—and it's also what they *want!*" But I don't. I decided to write this book, instead.

## Equity

To provide all students with a level playing field, there must be a pervasive belief that curriculum and instruction, opportunities and expectations, and protocols and procedures should be equitable for all students.

In addition, students need equitable access to a **culture of dignity** as well.

What does this look like within a school? For there to be equity, curriculum must be taught in a similar-to-identical fashion by all grade-level or content-specific teachers. Objectives and standards are mapped, paced, and adhered to. Best practice instructional strategies are taught to all staff; teachers are not left to seek out their own professional development that only impacts their growth (and not their colleagues).

Expectations for staff and students are common throughout the building, and these expectations are clearly articulated and taught to all stakeholders. We call this **purposeful redundancy**. Procedures within the building—anything ranging from teacher requests to high ability placements—are systematic and follow a set of prescribed protocols. Are there gaps? Absolutely! Are leaders continually required to meet, discuss, and seek out these gaps? You bet.

Evaluations are another area where similar-to-identical expectations are key. Each teacher is evaluated consistently with a common rubric regardless of who their evaluator is. (An example of the evaluation rubric, specifically the section on PLCs, is located on page B1 of the Appendix.) Administrators spend time calibrating their evaluations throughout the year and often questioning each other's interpretations of the rubric. The goal here is to provide students the opportunity to learn from the best teachers in the state—as teacher effectiveness increases year after year.

We know. Rules. Lists. Rubrics. Expectations. Sounds exciting, right? Ha! Oh, we've heard the questioning statements more than a time or two. Sounds more like a robotic camp where everyone had better fall in line. Sounds like a cold work environment where evaluations dominate much of the decision-making for teachers. Sounds like a difficult place to work.

Well, to be honest, yes—it is a difficult place for *some* people to work. We've actually grown to be completely transparent about this fact with all of our teachers, as early as the initial interview. To teach and thrive in Brownsburg requires that staff are willing to put their egos aside, receive feedback, work hard, and prioritize student learning. Over the years, dozens of previously highly effective teachers have joined our staff only to quickly realize that what was good enough somewhere else was simply okay in Brownsburg. Do you know how hard it is to hear that? It's awful. It's heart-breaking. And often, it's true.

Do we ask ourselves if it's worth it? Is it worth these tough conversations—year after year? Sure we do, and the answer is always yes. The proof is in the pudding; the sauce isn't secret—it all comes down to equity. When similar-to-identical approaches lead across an entire district, equity makes an indelible mark.

In Brownsburg, elementary school students all share an identical schedule in terms of time spent on varying subject areas. The reading block at Reagan is the same 90 minutes as the reading block at Cardinal. The intervention opportunities and strategies at Lincoln are similar to identical to those at White Lick.

As a learning specialist with a background in language arts, I often host writing-specific workshops at both schools and at our center. The top two common concerns that set off my alignment and efficiency radar? A lack of equitable (or common) instruction time for students and the absence of direct writing instruction in the schedule. The main issue at hand is a lack of common, equitable access to the content.

In *Belonging Through a Culture of Dignity: The Keys to Successful Equity Implementation*, authors Dr. Floyd Cobb and John Krownapple explain that, "For educational equity, access and belonging are both vital." To ensure a guaranteed and viable curriculum, as Robert Marzano also suggests, is to ensure equitable access to content. That's half of the educational equity coin.

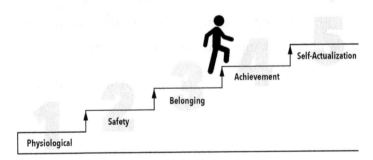

**Figure 2.1** Reprinted from *Belonging Through a Culture of Dignity* with permission from the author.

If the strategy of implementing identical schedules across buildings sounds simplistic to you, you would be right. The problem is that educational leaders all too often overlook the simple leverage points that create equity (i.e., common schedules that create equal opportunities for all students to access the curriculum).

## "A Bad System Will Beat a Good Person Every Time"

W. Edwards Deming was onto something quite extraordinary when he strung these words together. In 2010, unbeknownst to many of the good people working in Brownsburg, the systems of the schools were, well, bad. Again, this isn't to say that the school was low achieving or that the teachers were ill-prepared. In fact, the truth is quite the opposite. In 2010, nearly 82% of all Grade 3–8 students passed both their English and math state assessments. The graduation rate was 91%, compared to the state range of 78% to 88%. Teachers were generally well-liked and trusted by parents in the community. On the surface, Brownsburg Community School Corporation, or BCSC, was a good school system.

Perhaps, however, it is because of the mislabeling of schools as "good" that leaders in education are missing the key leverage points that propel schools into the "great" category.

Similar to identical, a system of systems, is that **leverage point.**

Table 2.1  Good vs. Great Leverage Points

| GOOD | GREAT |
|---|---|
| Teaching state standards, but no common curriculum | Similar to identical curriculum |
| Teacher autonomy | Teacher collaboration (PLC/Impact Teams) |
| Individual methods for lesson planning | Common language for lesson design |
| Limited vertical alignment of curriculum | Vertical alignment of curriculum |
| Individual, teacher-designed assessments | Common assessments |

Because autonomy ruled the day in Brownsburg, teachers within a building were left to make varying decisions all too often for their own benefits (instead of the students'). Sure, some teachers were highly effective rock stars and their lesson design and classroom culture did manifest themselves in student achievement on formal assessments, but there was no common measurement—no system—to help replicate their strategies.

This replication of best practices—that's the gold standard we should be after in education. Imagine a doctor discovering a cure for a disease but never sharing. Sound ludacris? The same is happening in education, in schools in all communities, and we have to address this issue.

In 2010, there was no common set of expectations guiding curriculum alignment, common assessments, aligned intervention, equitable access to programs, professional development, or building-level protocols. It's not to say these aspects of school leadership were missing entirely from the district, but there was not an agreed-upon belief that these systems should be common.

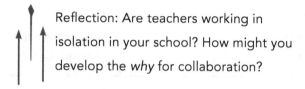

Reflection: Are teachers working in isolation in your school? How might you develop the *why* for collaboration?

## Year Two

At the start of Dr. Snapp's second year as the superintendent, it became apparent to all staff (especially his leadership team) that he was going to lead the district with a clear, streamlined focus. Countless programs across the district were eliminated, much to the chagrin of many staff members (some of whom had provided the "too many programs" feedback in the previous year). Initiatives that were stopped dead in their tracks included technology integration, special projects, PBL, cross-curricular units of instruction, required reading logs, and various building committees. The six elementary school principals were called together to create one, common schedule at all buildings. Instructional coaches were added at each elementary. Intervention periods were accessible to students in need at each building, K–8.

If the district had been a chalkboard, and initiatives had filled and erased, filled and erased, 2011 was the year that the board was actually wiped clean.

The three secondary principals were introduced to a new position, a **secondary department head (SDH)**, whose administrative goal was to align content areas in Grades 6–12—but especially 6–8. In addition to alignment, the goal of the curriculum area administrators was to serve as coach, evaluator, professional development guide, and hiring lead for their area of teachers. You can find SDH roles in the Appendix, page B2.

The high school principal absorbed the SDHs, as they were quickly nicknamed, and these curriculum leaders became an integral part of Dr. Snapp's leadership team somewhat overnight. One notable difference between these SDHs and typical department heads is that Brownsburg hires administrators to serve in these positions. This group joins the district leadership meetings and is parallel to the assistant principals, who largely work with students and parents. The SDHs, conversely, largely work with teachers and staff. We both serve (and served) as the science and English SDH, and essentially led as the instructional coaches for our content areas.

On a macro level, 2011 also brought about a district-wide vision of what professional learning communities would look like inside this district. Building leaders along with central office staff spent months in preparation studying the works of Richard DuFour and Mike Schmoker to determine the key components of the PLC system within Brownsburg.

Now, as I work with districts across the state who seek to implement PLCs with fidelity, I often hear stories of how entire administration teams fly to conferences to learn how to roll out PLCs. This approach is often great for leadership camaraderie building, but it fails to meet the implementation needs of a district.

How was Brownsburg different? Well, for starters, we didn't fly 50 of our leaders across the country to attend a workshop. Instead, they read and studied common resources; a list of books studied are in the Appendix on page B3; they met and discussed and planned. Throughout the school year, the district leadership team created a common, collective understanding of what PLCs would look like in their district, and only then were they ready.

If you do not have the staffing capacity within your district to create, coach, and lead a new system, consider your vetting process of determining which professional learning partners you bring in. In *Leading Impact Teams*, Bloomberg and Pitchford describe the intention of working with districts to "support schools by creating conditions where innovation and creativity thrive." At the end of the day, they believe in teacher collective efficacy, as do we, as the ultimate professional learning goal that impacts student learning. Be sure your professional learning team (if outside of your district) aligns with your learning beliefs.

In the summer of 2011, the first-ever PLC Leadership Summit was held, and all brand-new PLC leaders throughout K–12 were invited to attend. One note of clarification: PLC leaders are teachers in Brownsburg. We are not referencing the district admin team; we are referring to grade-level and content-area teachers who lead their peers each week.

The first summit was a two-day training on campus that provided the systematic approach to training all administrators and selected leaders to learn just exactly how Brownsburg would approach PLCs, data, curriculum, and assessments. The training also sent a clear message that in terms of professional development, Brownsburg was changing its system. Professional development would become an almost exclusively in-house affair, and requests to travel to local, state, or national conferences would now be denied.

Yes, I have to acknowledge the obvious elephant in the room: I am now a professional learning specialist. Such irony. I now serve as a leader responsible for professional learning events, yet I whole-heartedly encourage districts to develop district-wide plans for PD. I love to work with entire districts on vision, strategy, and PLC needs. You can bring someone in—that's no problem. And you can send someone to test the waters to see if a presenter is worth trusting and following (I totally get that). But it's less effective, by and large, to continue to send your teachers at-will to random workshops. That's not the strategy you want to use if you're trying to create similar-to-identical practices that impact student learning. Back to the process.

In 2011, the system for how to best support teachers in their professional learning communities was formed. All teachers, in all buildings, were allotted 45 minutes a week (either during an early release or late start) to meet with grade-level or content-area teachers. During this meeting, all teachers would essentially follow the same discussion format:

1. Celebrate
2. Share common data
3. Create response plans
4. Determine next objective, assessment, and response
5. Reflect

To say this new change was met with welcoming arms from all teachers would be a gross overstatement. There were pockets of teachers who had already been involved (at building levels) in what they called PLCs. Some of these teachers had the belief that their approach to curriculum and data was, in fact, sufficient. They didn't necessarily understand the purpose behind adding an agenda, or why everyone's agenda needed to look the same. An example of an agenda used in our district is on page B4 of the Appendix. Sound familiar? Schools are totally falling into these camps with PLCs. We see it all the time now. Trust us: wade through this muck. Give it time. Keep the expectations, norms, protocols, common meeting places. Oh yes, there was also the issue of where PLCs needed to meet.

In 2011, PLC meetings shifted from classrooms to common spaces like media centers or cafeterias. Some teachers were excited about the shared meeting time; others were skeptical. It was hard to explain to everyone why they needed to be together, in one space, to conduct these meetings. Some teachers argued that it was harder to focus with everyone in the same room. Some felt as if they were being watched or that administrators were keeping tabs on them. Still others were just uncomfortable with the entire process of sharing their data, period.

I was one of those teachers. It's comical now looking back, but it's true. In 2011, I was a brand-new PLC leader and I still remember the angst we felt about having to fill out an agenda (because who would be spying on us?) and then having to meet together (because don't they trust us as professionals?!) Also, I was a teacher leader at this time. I think back on my earlier teacher-self and am thankful to have had patient, steadfast leaders who nudged me along.

Implementing the system was not a smooth transition. If you had asked teachers in Brownsburg in 2011 if there was power in their PLC system, their responses would vary greatly. Changes don't often come easily, and perhaps this is why so many schools across the country have attempted and then failed to purposefully create PLCs in their buildings. Convincing an entire staff to want to collaborate, to want to be vulnerable—that's tough.

Convincing an entire district might seem downright impossible.

But again, that's where the naysayers would be wrong.

I currently coach and consult with schools where their baby steps have lasted 7+ years. And almost all-too-late the principals are realizing: we didn't hold the line because we didn't *create* the line. Give your teachers boundaries. Set the expectations. Hold the line. Rip the Band-Aid.

*Lead.*

## Alignment

It is precisely *because* staff in all buildings *were* held to the same expectations for PLC meetings and processes that there was the eventual (and dramatic) buy-in. There have been many widely accepted arguments in various forms of leadership literature that caution against a "top-down" approach to decision-making. Many of the world's most influential leaders—both past and present—are precisely thus because they did not make decisions in isolation; they drafted teams of highly skilled and passionate leaders to work alongside them to help implement their visions.

In regard to school district leadership, an important question must be asked if leaders are to gain any real traction with their teachers: Is it okay or even beneficial to need both a team of skilled leaders *and* top-down approaches? If, for just a moment, district leaders—and I am referring to superintendents here—begin to consider themselves the instructional leaders for their principals, teachers, and students, then what positive implications could this have for learning across their districts? What if this entire notion of "top-down" decision-making is mistakenly synonymous for a simpler, more celebrated term?

*Vision.*

Superintendents must wear many hats in order to adequately support all members of their staff. Still, the most important hat that any person working in education should wear is that of the instructional leader. The instructional leader is the visionary for the group of people—whether students or teachers—he or she leads. If superintendents are willing to see a vision of all teachers within their district embracing the process of professional learning communities; if all superintendents are willing to support their team of instructional leaders to buy-in to this same vision; if all superintendents are willing to stay focused, year after year, after year on this vision—then alignment will occur.

Without the vision, set from the instructional leader at the top, the system will be absent of alignment.

Grassroots movements that rely entirely on teacher-created momentum do not create systems. Setting a vision does not equate to leadership devoid of buy-in, but relying only on buy-in from all stakeholders is a common misstep in far too many districts.

In 2011, prepared with a clear vision of the power of professional learning communities, the superintendent in Brownsburg brought together his leadership team—principals, assistant principals, curriculum leaders, and data specialists—and together they planned how to take the vision and turn it into reality. For one year, Dr. Snapp and his leadership team read books, studied model schools, and discussed with great detail just exactly what they hoped to achieve through the creation of PLCs. Conversation after conversation was had. Viewpoint after viewpoint was considered. Plans began to develop.

By the spring, the leadership team had decided that in order to create the district alignment they sought they would host a PLC leader summit (an example agenda is in the Appendix page B5) over the summer. This laid the foundational groundwork for teacher-leaders throughout the district. It defined what PLCs would be in Brownsburg, clarified the *why* behind the process, and equipped teacher leaders with the tools they needed to guide their peers down this path.

Hundreds of teacher leaders across the district attended. The superintendent and his team of leaders designed an in-house professional development workshop with the goal of aligning vision and leadership in each of its buildings. Kindergarten teachers sat next to ninth-grade biology teachers. Music teachers sat beside core-content area peers. The goal of the summit was to educate every leader collectively on what the PLC process would mean in Brownsburg.

Several clear messages were created by simply hosting this initial summit.

- → **We have a common vision.**
- → **Everyone, at every level, is a part of this.**
- → **Everyone, at every level, is accountable.**
- → **Teacher leaders are valued and highly respected.**
- → ***This* is our professional development.**

Consider again for a moment how many districts approach professional development. Teachers are allowed to pursue their personal passion or growth areas, often attending conferences on their own accord. Districts afford a set amount of their budgets each year to provide these individual trainings to teachers. There might be some guidance given on which conferences to attend, or it might be entirely wide open for the teachers themselves to choose. Not all teachers will attend conferences, of course, so your staff is quickly made up of teachers who are "growing" and teachers who are "stagnant" in terms of their professional development via conferences and workshops.

For those who do attend outside trainings, perhaps some will be required to report back on what they experienced or learned. Perhaps they will lead a faculty meeting on innovative topics. Maybe they'll create and lead a book study. A small group. A webinar.

Then what?

The process begins again the following year, often creating a knowing–doing gap. And there's no way to systematically measure the effectiveness of attempted implementation of any one of those hundreds of strategies.

No one knows which strategy yielded the highest results, therefore no one knows what to replicate.

And now, I am part of this cycle! I know workshops are meaningful and impactful, but at the end of the day, I have a vision for equipping district leadership teams with the tools they need to align their visions and create a system that supports it.

The PLC leadership summit took the guesswork out of professional development—at least in terms of PD about professional learning communities. After that first summit, building PLC leaders were charged with the task of starting and leading groups of teachers in their buildings through the newly defined process.

That first summit created a common platform for the district leadership team to utilize in the years that followed. Brownsburg has since hosted this leadership summit for nine years in a row (and counting). Every summer PLC leaders across the district know that they will be asked to attend the in-house summit. They get paid a stipend for the day (money that used to be spent on substitutes or out-of-district conference fees) and Qdoba for lunch (extra queso, please). The leaders spend their mornings in heterogeneous groups outside of their own buildings while the afternoons are dedicated to building-specific PLC work. The forum provides ongoing alignment and support for veteran leaders as well as brand-new leaders. It also keeps the administrative team aligned in its interpretation of PLC best practice, growth areas, and next steps.

Some years the impact of the summit has been palpable among teachers and leaders, while other years . . . not so much. As members of the planning team, we reflect annually on what works and what doesn't for the summit. Throughout the year, the admin team studies various resources on PLC leadership, protocols, and group dynamics, and ultimately we hope to glean nuggets and takeaways that will meet the needs of our teachers. Some recent book reviews (see full PLC book list in the Appendix, on page B3) include:

→ *Leading with Focus*, Mike Schmoker
→ *Groups at Work*, Laura Lipton and Bruce Wellman
→ *The Five Disciplines of PLC Leaders*, Timothy D. Kanold

In addition, PLC notes are studied and reflected upon throughout the year. Below is a sample of meeting notes from a PLC:

BROWNSBURG COMMUNITY SCHOOL CORPORATION
SECONDARY SCIENCE PLC AGENDA & NOTES

DATE:                                          PLC:

| PLC/PGP GOAL | Building Goals |
|---|---|
|  |  |

**PLC Reflective Questions to Ponder/Guide You**

- What is a data strategy that will lead us to dig deeper into our data?
- How do we authentically reflect on our PLC process and student learning?
- How can you more closely tie your PGP "action research" to your weekly PLC process?
- How do we foster growth amongst each other and students through student-centered reflections/discussions in our PLC meetings?

**Celebrations**

**What Do We Want Students to Know?**

**How Do We Know That Students Have Mastered the Objective(s)?**

**What Will We Do With the Students Based Off Their Current Level of Mastery (Re-teach/Enrichment)?**

**How Will What You Did in PLC Today Impact Students?**

**Tasks for Next Time:**

The planning of the summit occurs while we're still busy running buildings and departments, so it isn't always clean and easy. And, we have to collaborate together—and we don't always agree. The intent isn't always clear, and conversations occur, reoccur, and reoccur again.

Last spring I met with Dr. Snapp to pick his brain about the summit preparation process. Our leadership team was half-way through a book study of his choosing, and I just really wasn't feeling it. Keep in mind, for many of us this was book five or six on effective PLC leadership, and I just didn't jive with the flow and content of the resource.

I also worried that we were shooting blind as a team. We started with the resource instead of starting with our intentions. What growth areas were we wanting to address via the summit? What nuggets were we seeking from the resource and why? The planning process just felt backwards.

Like our first meeting some nine years earlier, Jim came prepared to listen and brainstorm. He had a notebook and was ready to hear me out. He listened as I shared my questions and suggestions, and ultimately we came to a critical moment in the discussion when he asked, "What is the purpose of the summit?"

I paused, gathering up my various options. "Obviously," I slowly began, "we want to provide our teacher-leaders with tools they can use throughout the year."

He nodded.

"But beyond that, I think . . . the bigger purpose is to reiterate that PLCs are the main thing. They are what we do here. It's how we grow. They're our priority."

More nods.

"So, it's more about the global message of importance and less about the actual content each year. Though we do want each year to be awesome."

"Exactly," he replied. "Are there some years when our summit is better than others? You bet. That's never the intent, but that's reality. The purpose of the summit is to help keep the focus on PLCs."

I share this conversation for two reasons.

1.  How many leaders have open, constructive conversations with their superintendents about how they are structuring a process? Do we feel we are able to lead up—even if it means leading up to the top? Do our teachers feel the same way?
2.  Having an annual summit is the number one missing piece in districts that I currently work with. Leaders spend all of their time and energy getting a system off the ground, but they neglect to build in fail-safes that support the system.

At the time that this book is being written, Brownsburg has had over 100 different schools from across the state of Indiana visit to observe its PLC process and pick the brains of both administrators and teacher leaders alike. One key piece of the PLC puzzle is to implement a PLC summit—a common training for all leaders—and we share this nugget with all of our visitors. It is remarkable how many schools or districts have attempted to implement professional learning communities without first leading their leaders or articulating their vision.

If district leaders do not create a system where all parties are aligned in their understanding of the vision, you will not have true professional learning communities. Period.

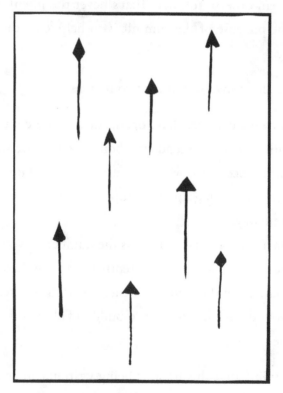

**Figure 2.2** Aligned Arrows within Districts

Alignment at the beginning of a process is a crucial, critical first step. If you've got all of your arrows pointing in the same direction, at the same target, your likelihood of hitting the target increases tenfold. And, you must retrain all new hires. Every. Single. Time.

But what do you do *after* the trainings—after your summit—to monitor alignment of your processes? What other systems are in place to support your teacher leaders throughout the entire year and to remain aligned with the vision? To keep the arrows moving in the right direction?

## Follow-Up Support Is Key

In order to provide continued support to teachers, Brownsburg schools have built in teacher support positions at various levels. The teacher support positions include instructional coaches at each elementary school; secondary department administrators for larger, core departments; as well as specialists that support populations of students with disabilities. There is also one main data analysis coordinator for the district who provides ongoing support to both teachers and administrators throughout the year.

The goal of these teacher support positions is to coach all teachers—including the PLC leaders—to make the best curriculum and instructional decisions possible to maximize student learning. In each meeting, teachers are asked to look at evidence, analyze this evidence, and decide upon necessary action steps. Bloomberg and Pitchford (2016) refer to this as the EAA protocol. DuFour & Eaker R. (2006) use four main questions to accomplish this task.

→ What do we want students to learn?

→ How will we know if they have?

→ What will we do, differently, to re-teach students who haven't mastered the objective?

→ What will we do to enrich the learning of students who have mastered the objective?

Teachers want to do their very best each day. They really do. Still, balancing all of the demands of the job can become overwhelming for even your highest-performing rock star teachers. When that happens, what supports do you have in place to meet each of your teachers where they are exactly at that moment?

By providing staff positions that are dedicated to coaching and supporting their teachers, Brownsburg has created a built-in follow-up to the PLC summit that ensures all teachers have the opportunities to receive instructional support from experts should the need arise. These instructional support roles may also ensure that PLC processes are followed efficiently within each group.

When you do have teacher support roles in place who are effectively coaching staff, those leaders must also work to communicate in abundance to principals and other building leaders. If a teacher or PLC is struggling, the principal and instructional coach must work together, with open communication, about how to best support the teacher(s). If they do not, the expectation for teacher or PLC effectiveness will be unclear and alignment is thrown off.

And your coaches must be aligned, too. Your curriculum team must know your mantras and vision and speak it with clarity. You would be amazed at how often leaders *believe* their people are all on the same page when in fact they are *not*.

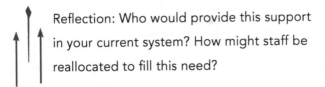

Reflection: Who would provide this support in your current system? How might staff be reallocated to fill this need?

## Goals

You would think that since we're talking about goals, we would have put this first on the list out of equity, systems, and alignment. After all, without clear goals how can the people within the system even know what they are aspiring toward? So, why put goals last?

It's simple: *goals change all of the time.*

Similar to identical creates a system. And remember, without a clear system of expectations and protocols, even the best people will fail.

The goal is not the desired outcome of achieving a certain sense of accomplishment each week during PLC meetings. The goal(s) must be specific, measurable, attainable, relevant, and timely (SMART). An example of our PGP (Professional Growth Plan) process can be seen in the Appendix on page B6.

School goals are incredibly important but quick to be forgotten. In fact, we would argue that the vast majority of teachers around the United States would be hard pressed to articulate even one of their many school goals. Recall my previous story about school improvement plans and my admin program. And how, we wonder, can a teacher reasonably stretch to achieve a goal they may or may not even know about?

On the other hand, both equitable curriculum decisions and aligned systemic practices can be made clear to all teachers year after year. Once established, they shouldn't change. When teachers operate within a system that utilizes aligned practices in all buildings, there is a sense of security and appreciation for this consistency. Consider the impact it makes on a second-grade teacher who finds out they will need to move buildings the next school year due to changes in enrollment. They do not have to worry about what curriculum, systems, or expectations are present at their new school because they are the same that were present at their old school. Will the culture of each building be slightly different? Oh absolutely, and we cannot imagine anyone arguing otherwise. Still, it's the systems and alignment that create the all-important sense of equity needed across a district if it is to truly thrive.

Determining a school's goals should occur only once the district as a whole has established its goals. After, each school's goals should feed into and support the district level. Once school goals are established, PLCs and individual teachers can create their own SMART goals that feed both school and district goals. Our PGP Goal Timeline and Steps are in the Appendix on page B6.

One crucial note of importance:

Keep your goals to a minimum if you want to maintain clarity and focus for your staff. Apply this same principle to your district if you want to create unity and cohesion among all teachers.

There is a sense of security and justice for staff when they know each school in their district is held to the same standards. Goals are a great equalizer when they are used as such. Goals also create opportunities for people to continually reflect upon what exactly they are doing—and for what intent and purpose.

If you want to articulate your district's goal-development beliefs, create a visual for all staff to reference.

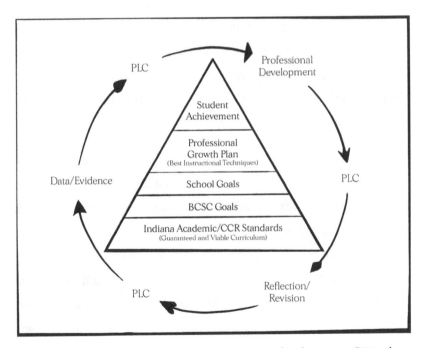

**Figure 2.3** Brownsburg's Goal Development *More details on page B7 in the Appendix

This visual was created by the administrative team in the district (principals, assistant principals, curriculum team, central office) and has been studied and revised several times since 2011, when it first appeared at the PLC summit. In a nutshell, the visual shows how the PLC process, added to a standards-based curriculum, drives all teachers' abilities to reach their student achievement goals. Note: Teachers have the instructional control. They create a bulk of their curriculum. Curriculum creation is not the issue. Curriculum implementation and fidelity are the issues.

John Hattie and Robert Marzano have conducted studies over the past 50 years to pinpoint which strategies present the highest yield in terms of student achievement. Consistently, two variables rise to the top: teacher effectiveness and a common and viable curriculum. In Chapter 7, we explore the processes used to grow and support teachers to be as highly effective as possible, but before we get there we'll first explore the power of having that common, viable curriculum at all buildings, grades, and content areas.

Though states clearly define standards for all content areas, far too many district leaders leave the curricular decisions entirely in the hands of individual teachers—meaning, teach or don't teach the standards. It's up to you. I have friends and family members who have shared specific conversations with principals who straight up told them, "I don't care what you teach as long as the kids are moving forward." Are you kidding me? As a parent, I would be irate to hear that my daughter's high school biology teacher didn't actually have to teach the standards—at least as far as the principal was concerned.

Apply this same ideal about autonomy to most other professions, and we're appalled. You'd never have an engineer who is given free reign on whether they follow the blueprints or not, or simply design based on gut instinct and previous experience. No way.

Teacher autonomy has become a tradable commodity in education. In an effort to recruit and keep effective teachers, curricular decisions are bargained—despite the fact that it's ultimately the students who pay the price of having inconsistent approaches to instruction.

Leaders, stop leveraging trust and respect as ways to disguise misalignment.

Autonomy, truly, is another word for inconsistency.

I recently joined a district leadership team to help them troubleshoot year two PLC roadblocks (plus unique teaching-in-a-pandemic questions). As we reviewed the list of concerns they had identified, gaps in Tier I instruction were at the top. They realized that because there had not previously been a guaranteed, viable curriculum in place, inconsistency in core literacy practices were dramatically impacting the data.

I celebrate this revelation made by these principals, because one of the first steps is to have the courage to confront what the data has shown. Their data, in this case, reflected the impact of allowing teachers autonomy in curricular decisions.

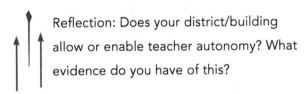

Reflection: Does your district/building allow or enable teacher autonomy? What evidence do you have of this?

# Chapter 3:
# People, Not Programs

"When the number of initiatives increases,
while resources and emotional energy
are constant, then each new initiative . . .
will receive fewer minutes, money, and
ounces of emotional energy."

– Doug Reeves

## Who Are Your Key Players?

RIGHT ABOUT NOW, YOU MIGHT be feeling excitement. You agree that similar-to-identical approaches are powerful ways to create equitably aligned systems that feed your district's (or school's) goals. You greatly admire and value your teaching staff, but you recognize the influence of a common, viable curriculum for your students. You know you are an instructional leader, and you are capable of making these shifts in philosophy occur in your schools. You are ready.

*But . . .*

You cannot do this alone.

As an instructional leader, your primary job is to guide learners in your sphere to think, question, and grow. Perhaps your learners are students. Perhaps they are principals. Regardless, it is your responsibility to create meaningful avenues of learning for your team—especially when considering philosophical decisions like curriculum alignment, the creation of PLCs, or the streamlining of goals.

So, how do we do this? How do we set the vision within ourselves, and then, without dominating, controlling, or cajoling, inspire the leaders of learning around us to jump on the bus?

How do we determine our key players in the game?

At the second **PLC leadership summit**, there was excitement and a bit of buzz in the air. State testing results had come in, and we were thrilled to learn that student achievement on both math and ELA tests had jumped considerably. We went from being ranked in the 20s and 30s in the state on these exams to 5th—in one year. We were beginning to see, as a district, the impact of PLCs and alignment, and we were asked to reflect on what brought us this success.

Dr. Snapp posted a list of potential reasons for our growth and success:

A.  **Common Writing Curriculum**
B.  **Improved Intervention Processes**
C.  **PLC Frameworks**

D. Narrowed School Goals

E. Outstanding People

F. All of the Above

In small groups we were asked to make the hard choice of determining exactly what brought about the success. Based on everything we've shared in this book up to this point, you might be like the majority of the room that day and choose F. I know my group did.

And much to our surprise, we were shocked to find that we were incorrect.

The reason for the success, Dr. Snapp claimed, was in fact the result of E—our outstanding people.

## Looking for Leaders

If you are the leader of a district, school, department, or group, you have to constantly ask yourself this question:

*How is my leadership serving the vision of our team?*

Think about that for a moment. If you've got a notebook handy, stop reading and reflect on that question. What do you think? On a scale of 1–10, where do you land? Perhaps you realize that your leadership serves the vision in certain circumstances but not others. What are the others? What are you doing that does not serve the vision? Why are you doing that?

In order for a systems-based philosophy to take hold, all leaders must—and we mean *must*—serve the vision of the district at all times. It is critical that your leadership team buys-in to the process. They will ensure that their teachers develop the buy-in, too. They will inspire, encourage, motivate, and ignite.

In a way, the leadership team is like the sales team. They are the face of the company—the ones everyone else looks to for assurance and confidence.

If your leadership team is not aligned, you will not create sustainable growth. Period.

And what does a misaligned vision look like? Eye rolling; winking; "we just have to" statements; blaming central office; blaming anyone.

## Your Leadership Team

Many superintendents are aptly cognizant of the number of meetings they ask their principals and administrators to commit to. Standard meetings with teachers, staff, parents, and students already fill a principal's day, so to request that administrators set aside additional time to meet with one another across the district might at first feel like you're asking too much of an already overloaded role. After all, a principal's primary purpose is to serve the students and staff of their building. Time spent away from the building equates to valuable time spent away from the people who need them the most.

Still, how can a superintendent ensure that all of their administrators—at all levels—have a common understanding of *how* to meet *which* needs if there is not built-in time set aside to bring together all the voices around the leadership table to, in fact, consistently align the vision? Starting with a clear, common vision is one thing; maintaining it in every aspect of your corporation, year after year, does not occur by happenstance or trust. This lack of purposeful redundancy in vision conversations is where the unravelling occurs. Superintendents can interpret quiet agreement as alignment, when in fact there is dissent.

You must inspect what you expect.

An unrelenting pursuit of alignment must occur between all roles and buildings; all leaders at all levels. You cannot remain in alignment if you do not bring your leaders together consistently throughout the year.

## Elementary

At the time that this edition was published, Brownsburg's enrollment had seen a steady increase in growth each year for eight consecutive years. This consistency in growth is the opposite of what most schools in Indiana have experienced. In 2018, Brownsburg opened its seventh K–5 elementary school. Census projections predict that an eighth and possibly ninth elementary might be in store for this community, but trends and predictions are not written in stone.

What is unique about Brownsburg's alignment in leadership is that each of the current seven (which could at one point become nine) elementary principals work in tandem with each other as an elementary team to ensure similar-to-identical practices in their buildings.

From daily schedules, to teacher interviews, to parent consent forms—the leaders of these buildings understand the importance of consistency among their buildings. When the district needs to hire elementary teachers, groups of these principals gather to conduct joint interviews of candidates. They utilize their collective hiring and leadership skills to pick out the absolutely best teachers for positions in each of their buildings. They respect the opinions of leaders in their sister buildings, and often they seek out critical feedback on their own ideas to ensure they are growing for the betterment of the staff they lead.

It's interesting. Leading at the elementary level can be one of the most rewarding but also challenging leadership roles for school administrators. On the one hand, students tend to be more naturally excited about school, life, and their teachers. Most want to please and follow expectations. It isn't as often that you must expel a student for drugs, fighting, or other offenses with legal implications. From the teaching perspective, elementary teachers tend to be creative, loving, energetic people who are 100% in the profession for the students (rather than, let's say, their content).

But there is a great deal of pressure to create success for students as young as possible, and research consistently shows that students who have not learned and mastered reading skills by the end of third grade will continue to fall behind year after year. If a student is not caught up and back to grade level benchmarks by sixth grade, it is nearly impossible to gain traction through middle school and high school.

In terms of pressure, the heat is most definitely on in the seven elementary schools within Brownsburg's district.

Because of the high expectations and tight building-to-building alignment, some school administrators would find it (and have found it) difficult to work within the system at Brownsburg. One of the reasons many outstanding teachers decide to leave the classroom to pursue a degree in school administration is because they view a school as an enlarged classroom. Principals are leaders because they are excited about the positive leadership and influence they can have on *their buildings*. For some, consistency and collaboration can quickly begin to feel like nit-picking and micromanagement.

Questions might arise like, "Why can't I just lead my building the way I best see fit?" or "I am the one who was hired to do this job, was I not?"

As a superintendent, you walk a fine line between balancing the needs of all of the stakeholders in the district and balancing the needs of your leaders who will execute your vision. Without the right leaders, your vision will lead to a dead end every time.

At the elementary level, it is important to seek out leaders who believe in the power of the group over the power of the individual. Whether your district has two elementary schools or 100, your success of implementing a common vision will depend on the alignment of beliefs and values among your leaders, and this starts with your elementary principals. Are your principals willing to set their egos aside to learn from new, up-and-coming leaders? Are they aware that their school serves a greater community, therefore the alignment of programs with sister schools creates ease for transient families? Are they maximizing support services such as special education, transportation, nursing, foods, and grounds by keeping a similar-to-identical mantra?

Are they willing to truly put themselves second to put the group first?

Find these leaders. They are out there. They may not be your current principals, and this is a hard pill to swallow. Then set aside *time* and create the *expectation* that these collaborative leaders work together each and every day. It should be a norm that principals call each other to run through questions about student discipline or teacher evaluations. It should be expected that principals have the same expectations for counselors and instructional coaches, building to building. These leaders are craving a cohort of exceptional peers that they can lean on to best lead their buildings. Provide today's principals with these opportunities to connect and thrive by setting aside meeting space where you consistently bring this team together. Require them to be their own PLC.

## Secondary

Middle schools and high schools tend to be larger in size and enrollment than elementary buildings. Fewer buildings means fewer principals. Often because of the age of the student, more assistant principals, deans, and curriculum leaders are needed to provide appropriate supports for students and teachers alike.

While you might not need to align as many principals at a secondary level, you do need to question how you are building capacity within all of your administrators to maintain and execute your vision. Does your middle school athletic director understand the intent behind your PLC process each week? Do your high school deans view themselves as instructional leaders as well as student liaisons? Are your multiple middle schools aligned in their course offerings, clubs, and experiences? Are you maintaining the momentum of learning experiences from K–5, or are you allowing variance to cloud the best execution of impactful practices?

When your secondary principals work together in alignment, congruence and trust become the norms of the district. When secondary principals are left to their own devices, the following scenario all too often occurs. For all intents and purposes, pretend you are the principal in this situation:

> It's 8:15 a.m., and the first-period bell rang only 25 minutes ago. You're just sitting down to check your email for the morning, and you notice a concern from a parent of a ninth-grade student. The parent's email is polite and succinct, but essentially there is a question about the rigor of what is being taught in his daughter's biology class. You notice that this parent didn't actually send you the email directly, but your teacher, Mrs. Martin, did. She is well-known in the building as a rock star, even though she's only in her second year at the high school. Just as you begin to file the email, you hear a rap at your door, and sure enough—it's Mrs. Martin. "I just don't know what you expect me to do!" she pours out the moment she steps in front of your desk.
>
> "How can I make this curriculum more rigorous when it's my job to teach the standards that align to the Biology end of course assessment?" She looks at you for a response. You nod;

she continues. "When I started with biology last year, there was no curriculum, no syllabus, no common assessments— nothing! The previous teacher left her class set of textbooks and some old scantrons—but that was it. I have spent the past year and a half creating a course from scratch—just to ensure our ECA scores remain high and the school's accountability scores are strong—and then I receive emails like this from a parent who clearly doesn't know anything about my content area!" She looks at you. Another nod. She continues.

"Here's why I'm actually frustrated, though—and this is a real kicker. This parent isn't wrong." You tilt your head forward— this ought to be interesting.

"His daughter is bored. I see it every day. She frequently tells me that she learned this material last year, in eighth grade, when she had Mr. Walsh." It's all becoming clear to you now. The root issue. You've heard it before. She says what you've known to be true for far too long:

"There's just no alignment."

Aligning the elementary schools in your district is the foundation of the house of learning you are building, year by year for each of your students. The next essential step is to ensure alignment at your secondary schools, as well. Many of the upper-level, college readiness classes require specific sequencing of courses for students to have adequate preparation. Without the alignment of curriculum and assessments, there's no telling if a student's previous course actually did prepare them or not.

It's also crucial that upper-level teachers trust the work that has been done before them in their content areas. In Brownsburg, we often tell our teachers that a teacher is allowed to teach whatever they want to their students—as long as they promise to teach that exact same group the following year, and the year after that, and the year after that. If you are the only one delivering instruction about your content—then no, you don't need to worry about aligning your curriculum because you are the gatekeeper extraordinaire of your content for these students. But, say you are like most other teachers in the United States; chances are you don't actually follow your students throughout their entire educational career.

Enter the need for alignment, vertically and horizontally, for all curriculum in all content areas. Teachers need a common curriculum to guide student outcomes, and students need this common curriculum so that their learning can build, year upon year. This stacked approach is especially beneficial for students with learning disabilities who might struggle with comprehension and vocabulary skills. When teachers use the same common terms (again, because of the prioritized alignment), students are able to use energy that might have been spent on memorization of new terms and apply this more readily to analysis and application skills.

In 2011, Brownsburg Community Schools created a unique leadership position, Secondary Department Head. Recall, the SDH position is a Grades 6–12 content area administrator whose responsibility includes creating and maintaining this alignment for teachers. What's unique about the SDH position is that these administrators are responsible for curriculum and instruction, yet they are not housed at the Central Office. The SDHs are curriculum leaders who float between the middle schools and high schools, working with principals to support teachers in core subject areas to maintain true alignment. Typically, curriculum leadership positions are reserved for Central Office positions, but as we'll next explore, the Central Office within Brownsburg looks slightly different from school systems similar in size.

Aside from all of the curricular leadership needed at the secondary level, it's also important that leaders of young adults make it a priority to put the students first in their decision-making. Look for secondary principals whose main purpose in education is to serve students, not themselves. You might think, "Well *of course* I want those kinds of leaders! Aren't we *all* supposed to have that view?" and of course your thoughts are spot-on.

The reality of the situation, however, is that far too many secondary leaders have been gifted their positions some years ago, and they themselves have lost touch with their students' perspectives on learning. Seek out leaders who love and embrace middle school crazy. Find high school principals who understand how stressful it is for today's teens to balance home, school, work, passion, and their futures. Do not settle for leaders who do not truly love their age group of students. Help these leaders find a position more properly suited for their mindset.

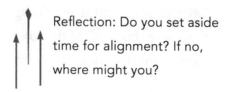

Reflection: Do you set aside time for alignment? If no, where might you?

## Central Office

Rounding out the leadership team is none other than the folks over at Central Office. There is an important concept that we suggest you adhere to when determining your needs at CO: Keep the decision-making in the hands of those closest to implementing the decision. When at all possible, we believe teachers should be the decision makers in regard to curriculum and assessment, and trusted instructional leaders within the buildings, not Central Office, should support the teachers in implementing these decisions. Instructional coaches and secondary department heads support teachers more readily than curriculum directors at the Central Office. Curricular implementation needs the support of a trained coach, and directors in Central Office positions, even at the smallest districts, are often viewed as a step too far removed from the classroom and building to be trusted on a coaching level.

Regardless of your size and which positions you do determine are necessary at the Central Office level, these leaders should be as integrated into the creation and implementation of the common vision as the principals and building leaders.

One of the ways you can ensure this alignment is to have regular, monthly meetings with your Central Office team and building-level principals. Make it a priority for the director of transportation, your CFO, and director of nutrition services to meet with building-level leaders. Can you find times throughout the year where these non-curricular experts can teach and train the building leaders?

Also consider ways that all leaders, including your Central Office administrators, strive for goals that align to the central vision of the district. The director of grounds and facilities should believe in your academic goals just as much as your principals and teachers. Do you require that all leaders regularly submit reflections on their goals with data to support their progress? How do you evaluate your leaders, especially at CO, to assess the impact of their leadership on the organization?

If you want to cement the importance of your leaders at the Central Office, first determine that every single role is critical and then have the people in these roles build authentic relationships with building leaders. To do this, we recommend allocating money for a leadership retreat every summer to kick off the start of the school year. This provides your team a much-needed opportunity for camaraderie to develop. Too often, leaders at the Central Office feel removed from the classroom and day to day events of their schools. Providing this collaboration between Central Office and building leadership is a necessary investment that creates cohesiveness for superintendents.

## Leaders Must Align

We've determined the importance of getting all of your leaders, at every level, aligned with common goals and structures that will simplify the execution of actions across the district. The other piece to the leadership puzzle is you want to find and cultivate a leadership team that can hold two opposing views together about leadership at the same time:

1.  It is vitally important to the structure of the organization that I see myself as one piece of a bigger picture.
2.  No other leader in this district can provide the insights and perspective that I can. I am an invaluable piece, and I have specialized information to share.

Are we suggesting that the best leaders can simultaneously know they are expendable and also irreplaceable at the same time? Absolutely! Is this easy? Absolutely not!

Each of your leaders is needed to create the whole, and the sum is greater than each of its parts. But, each of the parts has a unique leadership quality and perspective to share, so every leader on your team should feel valued and supported enough to know they add something to the team that no one else can quite replicate. Could the team go on without me? Yes, yes of course it could and it should. But am I the same leader as everyone around me—and should I be? No.

Because of our system, leaders tend to easily transition into our district or new roles. We do not hire leaders with the expectation that the person has all of the answers on day 1; we hire leaders with the expectation that they will be open to learning the system from the people who surround them.

You need a variety of thinking hats on your leadership team, and we would argue this applies to both district and school-level teams. So, even though we have spent a great deal of time (and will continue to do so) advocating for the power of being similar to identical and creating alignment, we still also believe in the power of avoiding groupthink. You need a variety of strong leaders, with unique talents and strengths, who all agree to join the same team to fulfill a clear vision.

Then, go find the best-possible teachers out there.

## Hire Great Teachers

We could honestly write an entire book about how to qualify what makes a great teacher and, in fact, braver educators than ourselves have already done so.

According to John Hattie (2003), the number one determining factor for a student's success in school is the strength of their teachers. There's a quote stolen from Todd Whitaker's *What Great Teachers Do Differently* that we whole-heartedly believe in here in Brownsburg: "It's about people, not programs."

People, not programs, make the difference. People, not programs, call home to check on students when they're sick. People, not programs, give kids hugs when they return to school. People, not programs, cry when they watch their toughest student beam as they walk the stage on graduation day.

People, not programs, are what students—in every single school—desperately need.

What can schools and districts do to find, recruit, and hire the top talent in the field? If location were not a factor (and let's be 100% transparent when we admit that yes, it is), what can and should schools do to market themselves to teachers in such a way that they are growing their bench with staff who also know the clarity of the vision and are excited to join?

Finding quality candidates who are willing to move to smaller, rural schools is absolutely a challenge. Finding quality candidates who are willing to serve more underprivileged populations is also a challenge. Keeping quality teachers in the classroom for more than four or five years is yet another obstacle to overcome. But if you can create a system in your district that empowers your leaders to seek out the absolutely best teachers available, and then enrich the interviewing process by following agreed-upon protocols, you will be one step closer to securing these candidates when they do come your way.

And then we need to consider the current climate of teaching during a pandemic. Joining a new school can be stressful enough without the uncertainty of changing learning environments and unpredictable health concerns. What can ease this stress? Collaboration. Common curriculum, assessments, and expectations. Why? Because as a new teacher to a system, I don't need to spend all of my time figuring out what to teach, which means I can spend more of my time figuring out *how* to be engaged and teach my students, regardless of their learning environments.

If you're like us, you'll be surprised to learn that like curriculum, much of the hiring decisions in school districts are left entirely up to each building principal. From screening to background checks, principals are often given complete freedom to hire who they want, how they want. Of course, the principal should have the most input on who is entering their building to teach their students, but in the end it's important to look above that singular building and create a system of protocols followed by all principals and administrators responsible for hiring. Just as a common curriculum creates equity and clarity for teachers, common hiring practices create a platform for administrators to agree upon the qualities they are searching for (or attempting to avoid) in potential teachers. An example of our hiring process can be found in the Appendix, on page C1.

In short, have a system. We recommend including various rounds in your interview process, allowing for multiple administrators or teacher-leaders to provide their various opinions on the candidate. When possible, include a model lesson round or require the teacher to actually teach to a group of students (an example of our model lesson instruction sheet is in the Appendix on page C2). Have consistent questions that you and your staff attempt to ask each interviewee, as that will allow you to compare responses. Teachers are a phenomenal resource when it comes to creating said questions, so look to your internal leaders to provide support if needed. And again, have these conversations on a consistent basis with your hiring team. Your human resource director should not be the only person in your district well-versed in best-hiring practices. Equip all leaders responsible for hiring to make their best-possible decisions for each and every candidate they seek to hire.

Reflection: Does your district have a common hiring process? How do you ensure equitable quality of hires between all of your schools? Are you asking questions that allow you to seek out highly effective teachers? How do you know?

Chapter 4:

# Tight-Loose-Tight

"When a teacher teaches, no matter how well
he or she might design a lesson, what a child
learns is unpredictable. Children do not
always learn what we teach. That is why the
most important assessment does not happen
at the end of the learning—it happens during
the learning, when there is still time to do
something with the information."

– Dylan William

IF A STUDENT WAS GOING to have the same teacher for all 13
years of their education, in all subject areas, the topic of common
curriculum would be a moot point. As the lone teacher, you can
ensure that each year your content is building upon the previous
year of instruction; there is continuity, clarity, and focus.

However, we do not teach and learn in a vacuum. A typical student in our current system will have upwards of at least
13 different English teachers throughout their K–12 educational
career—and that's *if* they have consistent teachers each semester

throughout high school. If you leave all curricular decisions to the teachers, that would mean that this one student might learn 13 different interpretations of how to write a thesis statement or analyze a text. And that's only if we consider English—let alone all of the other content areas impacting their learning.

There is a philosophical approach to curriculum that is referred to as "Tight-Loose-Tight," and we borrow it from Curriculum Management Audit. The concept of Tight-Loose-Tight is a transformative belief about curriculum and instruction that will have profound benefits on both teacher effectiveness and student achievement.

## A Common Definition

In *Good to Great* (2001), James Collins describes the idea of organizations keeping protocols and expectations tight. His phrasing for the balance of structure and autonomy is "Tight-Loose-Tight." This mantra of Tight-Loose-Tight creates a sense of "directed empowerment" according to Robert Waterman, author of *The Renewal Factor: How the Best Get and Keep the Competitive Edge* (1987).

Tight-Loose-Tight is a phrase used within Brownsburg schools to describe a common approach to curriculum. What teachers teach—the standards and objectives (and in what order, and for how long)—is the first Tight. This chapter will dive further into the processes used to guide the creation of this curriculum, but essentially what you teach should not be optional. The final Tight refers to agreed-upon common assessments for all students to complete in this curriculum. An assessment can take on various shapes and sizes, and effective instruction requires that students are assessed in a variety of formats. However, to ensure equity and relevance in regard to usable data, teachers in the same course should use the exact same common assessments—both formative and summative—to check their students' understanding. The curriculum is tight; the assessments are tight.

Table 4.1   Variety of Assessments

| Formative Examples: | Summative Examples: |
|---|---|
| Cold Call, White Boards, Four Corners, Exit Tickets, Polls, Muddiest Moment, etc. | Project, Lab Experiment Conclusion, Presentation, Graphic Organizer, Portfolio, etc. |

So, what's the Loose?

Thankfully, all teachers are different and bring their own unique personalities and skill sets to their students. Students *need* teachers who approach content differently so that they can have a chance to think about information in new, exciting ways. The best school leaders understand the importance of having a variety of strengths in their teaching staff, and these leaders look for ways to cultivate and embrace these differences. The Loose in Tight-Loose-Tight is the teacher's own unique approach to delivering the content, designing their lessons, and managing their classroom.

If the Tights are the science, the Loose is the art.

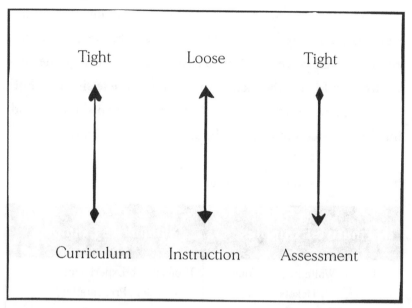

**Figure 4.1** Tight-Loose-Tight

Figure 4.1 is the best, most simplified approach to developing curricular approaches to serve all students. If equity is what you seek, a common, viable curriculum is needed in all subjects, at all levels.

## A Common, Viable Curriculum

Within Brownsburg, the framework of Tight-Loose-Tight guides the development of both primary and secondary curriculum. Teachers (yes, teachers) at the elementary and secondary levels are responsible for working together in teams (either by grade level, by PLC, or on appointed district-wide committees) to review standards, objectives, and teaching materials for each course.

Together, the teachers (we repeat this again) are responsible for determining the curriculum for their courses.

We go back to the philosophy from Chapter 3, "People, Not Programs." Teachers are the experts in their field, and when given the appropriate guidance, expectations, and time to develop quality curriculum, they will do so. If a curriculum is not standards-based or of high quality, then the ultimate blame should fall upon building and district leaders for failing to provide guidance and the time needed to create an aligned curriculum.

If you are currently allocating professional development money to send teachers away to various conferences, we would encourage you to greatly rethink this practice. Instead of sending teachers out, bring them in, together, in grade-level or content-area groups. Create a process for them to determine the most critical standards and objectives to teach and align (the Tight) and then allow them to make decisions. Rather than sending teachers out to learn a flavor-of-the-month technique, design a curriculum development process to be followed within your district. Teach your teachers how to do this. Lead by example and facilitate these workshops yourself. Hire consultants who can assist you in this if curriculum development is not your strength. Regardless of how you do it, reallocate your dollars to bring your people in, not send them out.

## In-House Professional Development

Once you have decided to spend your professional development money on your teaching staff (instead of on presenters from anywhere and everywhere), we recommend that you group teachers by grade and content, and then plan one to three in-house professional development days throughout the year.

The size of your district will determine the size of your groups. If you are a larger district, set aside grade-specific days where all of your second-grade teachers, for example, come together. We recommend building in a full day in the fall, a half day in the winter, and potentially a full day in the spring. When new curriculum is either adopted (which we'll explain next) or created (which we'll explain later), teachers need time together to fully unpack the expectations and understand the standards, objectives, outcomes, and pacing requirements—all before they can begin to design high-quality lessons.

These in-house professional development days ensure that all teachers in a common grade or content area are receiving the same information about the best practices that align to the vision of the district. Common professional development creates more common philosophies and understandings of the curriculum. A common understanding of the curriculum creates equity for students. No one teacher has the liberty to decide, "I think I'll just skip this unit this year," leaving the students in that room to suffer the consequences. Common professional development intends to level the playing field for all teachers, reiterate expectations in regard to curriculum and instruction, and raise the tide of all ships for all students.

One potential stumbling block to consider is how you will systematically support your small teams such as related arts and special education. When you have groups of teachers and staff who have unique content areas or roles, it can be challenging to create meaningful professional development that meets their needs. The challenge, however, should not exclude these groups from the benefits of responsive professional development. You may have pockets of teachers or staff who do not need professional development on as common of a rotation as your core groups, but we would caution you from overlooking them entirely. All teachers deserve the right to receive meaningful feedback and growth opportunities.

## Curriculum Adoption

In most districts, curriculum materials are typically adopted on a rotation. In Brownsburg, new books and curriculum are chosen every six years. At the seven elementary schools, teacher volunteers are chosen to be grade-level representatives on a curriculum adoption committee. These teams are designated in the spring for the upcoming year, and then final changes are made in the fall when the process formally begins. Teachers work together to determine the standards and outcomes the content will focus on and then the materials that might best meet their needs. Once the committee of teachers has selected its favorite materials, a parent approval round begins. Parents of current or upcoming students from the community are invited to weigh in on the curricular materials before the final steps of seeking approval from the school board. For every curriculum adoption rotation, this process is strictly followed. After the materials have been board approved, every elementary is expected to use the adopted materials with fidelity through the cycle.

In some districts, it is the coordinator or director of curriculum who facilitates this process. In Brownsburg, it is the assistant superintendent of curriculum and instruction. With the guidance and the assistance of instructional coaches and department heads, the teachers and parents in the community determine new learning materials each cycle.

The secondary process is similar to the elementary process. After evaluating the success of past curriculum adoption materials—identifying their strengths and weaknesses—departments work to set a vision for new potential curriculum needs. Departments work in teams to select and review materials before requesting parent review and input as well. Materials are vetted and questioned, often for the length of entire school years. Feedback and concerns are then sent to the assistant superintendent before materials are formally submitted to the school board for approval.

A core curricular belief in Brownsburg is that the people closest to implementing a change—or in this case, curriculum—should be the ones making the decisions whenever possible. We believe it is ineffective practice for district leaders to make sweeping curriculum decisions for teachers. After all, it's the kindergarten teacher who has to use that Basal reader, not the superintendent or director of curriculum. Teachers are the experts, and teachers should have the authority and trust to make these decisions with appropriate guidance and processes.

Once the book/curriculum adoption process has been followed, training and professional development hours should be set aside for all teachers who will use this new curriculum. We recommend that schools pay their teachers to unpack standards and write new curriculum in the summer. This allows teachers the chance to dive into the materials and assessments without the pressure of decision-making. Teachers can process and dialogue; they can propose and debate. Together, they can brainstorm, eliminate, and create. When the school year begins, a simplified, easy-to-follow pacing guide (or curriculum map) should be given to every teacher in this adopted content. Again, the curriculum is the first Tight in *Tight-Loose-Tight*. Once it's decided upon, all teachers should teach it with fidelity.

But having an agreed-upon map without the support of ongoing professional development and coaching can prove to be problematic. First of all, it's easy to agree on a curriculum when you're away from the daily grind of your students and your classroom. What sounds like a great plan in June might turn ghastly in a moment in September. Without a support system for teachers, curriculum can easily be abandoned or—worse—individually "tweaked" based on the emotionally reactive feelings of the teacher.

The professional development is the guidance on how to best implement the curriculum; in essence, the support of the Loose part of *Tight-Loose-Tight*. Though all teachers bring varying strengths to their classrooms, the best teachers believe in a relentless pursuit of excellence in terms of instruction and student learning. Tailored professional development, support that is responsive to your staff's particular curriculum and needs, is the best kind of training you can provide.

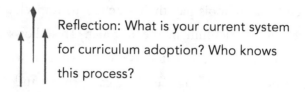

Reflection: What is your current system for curriculum adoption? Who knows this process?

## How Loose Is the Loose?

Tight-Loose-Tight is a guiding philosophical concept that has the power to transform the teaching and learning environments in an entire district. A solid, common curriculum that is assessed by high-quality, rigorous assessments should be an absolute priority for all schools.

But what about the Loose part of *Tight-Loose-Tight*?

We shared our case about the positive impact of systematic, in-house professional development, but what about individual teacher autonomy, creativity, and risk-taking? Are teachers in this system actually allowed to question the curriculum once it has been established? Can they ever try a new lesson—one that is not predetermined by the team, map, or pacing guide? What if they are the only teacher on the team to try this new approach . . . and it flops? Did they fail to meet the high expectations of the group? Were they careless, selfish, or nonconformist?

In a system of high expectations and what can feel like rigidity, some teachers rightly wonder, "Is there room in here for *me*, too?"

## The Art of Teaching

The Loose part of *Tight-Loose-Tight* is where all the magic happens, and after the planning processes are all over and done, this is where teachers and leaders need to live and breathe. Teaching is an art that the very best are called to perform. The goal of the leader should be to create a system that provides teachers the clarity needed to craft truly innovative, engaging lessons.

An aligned curriculum followed by aligned common assessments allows teachers the creative space to prepare the highest-quality lessons they can design. When a teacher is free from the hamster-wheel of, "What am I teaching next?" they are able to devote their energy toward the lesson, the questions, the discussion. Teachers are artists, and artists live to create. Some of the most creative strategies and lessons have been developed by our teams only after the common curriculum and pacing have been established. Teachers begin to authentically grow with one another as they explore their highest-leverage strategies. They challenge each other and question decisions; they evaluate their own effectiveness as a team as measured by student achievement gains. They dig into the weeds of how to best create the learning moments, the magic phrases, the "aha!" moments.

Consider, also, the impact that Tight-Loose-Tight can have on support staff. If all fifth-grade math classes are in the same unit, your inclusion and English Language Learner teachers are able to more readily shift from one class to the next, co-teaching alongside the Gen Ed teacher. Since the *what* of the curriculum is predetermined, both teachers can invest time in developing how it is best taught. Responsive in-class interventions best support *all students*, not only students who have IEPs. Teachers are begging for more time together to plan high-impact interventions and strategies. They desperately want to figure out what it is their kids need—so let's get out of the way! Give the teachers this time back by taking curriculum development off of the plate each week.

## The *A* Word

Assessment has become a semi-dangerous buzzword in education. We are living through an educational culture where high-stakes testing is a vital element of our system. Regardless of your personal feelings about standardized testing, we must agree that the prevalence of testing in our schools has created a shifting focus for many educators. State and national assessments in elementary, middle, and high school can strongly dictate curriculum and lesson design, and if left unchecked, entire pockets of educators will either respond in one of two ways.

Without expectation or proper guidance, some teachers may choose to simply ignore the benchmark assessments altogether. We have had multiple conversations with teachers, principals, and district leaders alike who readily admit that they choose to ignore everything about their state or national standardized tests. In an odd way, these educators often seem boastful about their decisions to rebel against the system. By claiming to devalue the importance of the standardized tests, educators in this type of culture actively bury their heads in the sand, so to speak, when it comes to analyzing the value or merit in such assessments. They also wash their hands of all responsibility, to both the students and their community in regard to results.

The lack of accountability to students and community is precisely the issue with this ostrich-like approach to standardized testing. Across the United States, students are ill-prepared for their state and national exams.

What's worse than the lack of preparation? More often than not, it's the teachers who are readily choosing to ignore the standards and skills that need to be taught to actually assist the students. If I don't teach it, I can't be held accountable for my students not learning it. It's suddenly no longer my responsibility. And who loses out year after year? The students.

On the other hand, teachers can also become hyper aware of the testing requirements, so much so that they begin to only teach to the test. Dynamic class discussion is replaced with rote online practice of "skills" needed to "pass the exam." There is a growing misconception that there is "testing" thinking, reading, and writing and then there is "real-world" thinking, reading, and writing.

This of course is absolutely absurd. The tests attempt to assess students' genuine abilities to read and think critically in any situation. There is no test in the system that *wants* students to write with less authenticity or weaker skill sets, but again and again we see teachers mistakenly teaching tricks and quick tips on how to write for a test. What happens? The writing is boring because the students are bored.

## Finding the Sweet Spot

If ignoring the test sets the students up for failure, but overly preparing for the test bores them to tears, then what's a teacher to do? Where's the happy medium? What strategy or set of strategies for testing and assessment are just right?

When you build a common curriculum that is based on the critical standards and skills addressed by these assessments, you have an unquestionable foundation that every lesson taught is preparing the students for the test. Each objective, every day, points to a specific, critical standard or skill, and these lessons build upon one another to authentically teach the content. An example of DOK (depth of knowledge) question stems is in the Appendix on page D1. This can be used when aligning the depth of thinking on standards, lessons, and assessments.

Teachers, principals, and district leaders *need* to know what's on the test so that they can design curriculum that aligns to the end assessment. In her 2011 book, *Making Classroom Assessment Work,* Anne Davies calls this philosophy of instruction and assessment, "beginning with the end in mind." You build curriculum with standards that are addressed on the end assessment. In our reality, the end assessment is often a state or national measurement.

We shouldn't feel guilty by examining the pieces of these state or national assessments. As teachers, we aren't teaching to a test; we are examining the structure that questions will present themselves in and we ensure that our level of questioning aligns appropriately to the expectations.

If, as the classroom teacher, I know the way questions are formatted, written, and presented, then I can infuse the content of my course to mimic the format. I am not attempting to prepare for a test, but I am aligning my questioning to a final product that in reality, my students *are* responsible for. Pretending the test does not exist is like pretending there are no parking spots in a parking lot. It is helpful to the students to know where they are going and how they'll need to "park their cars."

Equally as important as summative assessments are the day-to-day checks, or formative assessments. Examples of a summative and formative assessment can be found on pages D2 and D3 of the Appendix. If you are someone who interviews prospective teachers, be sure to ask questions about how this person knows their students are learning. Engagement and checks for understanding are the two most important elements of effective teaching, and a solid teacher will artfully explain how they know their students are truly learning.

Effective checks for understanding go well beyond the standard answers of "Exit Tickets." Teachers need to keep a constant pulse of how all learners are progressing through a lesson, discussion, lab, project, or reading. Frequent pauses in the process allow students to discuss, reflect, write, and respond. The purpose of a lesson is to call learners to think and grow, so as teachers we must provide them multiple opportunities each day to pause, think, and respond.

One misstep that often occurs is a teacher assuming that all students have thought through a question or problem, when in reality, only a handful in the room have done so. You've probably seen the following situation play out in at least one classroom in your building:

> Mr. Warner models the process for a new math problem on the board. Students have paper out in front of them, but only about half are taking notes. Occasionally, the teacher pauses and asks, "Make sense?" or "Understand?" and a few students in the room nod while the rest remain unmoved. The room is quiet, and Mr. Warner sees some students participating, so he reasons that students are listening and engaged. With each question he asks, he gets three or four raised hands, which shows that some students are interested. At the end of the practice, he assigns 15 problems to work on for homework and begins to circulate to answer one-on-one questions for students who ask for help. Many students around the room begin to raise their hands for help, and Mr. Warner works at a fast pace to answer each of their questions. When time runs out, five hands are still up as the bell rings.

Is Mr. Warner an effective teacher? We have no idea, and we don't propose that anyone could answer that question from just one snapshot into his class. What we can tell you is that while he believes he is checking the understanding of his students, in reality he is not. So many teachers believe that a quietly compliant classroom is an engaged classroom, thus learning must be occurring. Teachers mistakenly believe that students understand simply because no questions are raised. We argue quite the opposite.

When all students are expected to connect and understand the material, the guessing game of "Who really understands what?" is eliminated.

In his book, *Teach Like a Champion,* Doug Lemov references the importance of checking for understanding from 100% of your students. In a recent tweet, Lemov shares that, "Asking 'Everybody got that?' is one of the most common verbal habits of the teacher. We should just realize that the answer is almost never correct." We couldn't agree with him more.

We believe that one of the biggest mistakes is the teacher's failure to check for understanding from 100% of their students. Every single student should be asked to stop, write, discuss, and think. If you can hear or see the thinking, from 100% of your students, you can make an accurate decision on what to do next in your lesson.

Persida and William Himmele's book *Total Participation Techniques* is a great resource to use in all levels and courses. It provides 51 different total participation techniques, or TPTs, that help teachers quickly assess 100% of their students' understanding. Teachers want a variety of strategies to pull from, and this resource has ideas that will match each teacher's unique style. Formative assessment doesn't have to be complicated or flashy— it just has to be meaningful and accurate.

Are there ways to check *some* on your students' progress but not all—and still determine if you should move on, go back, or stay put? Absolutely. Poll your students by peppering perhaps one-third of them with the same repeated question. You aren't listening for the right answer and then moving on; you're taking a quick poll to hear, on average, how close they are to figuring out the correct answer.

Continual checks for understanding—questions, reflection, discussion—are vitally important in every single classroom at every single level. Our main priority in the classroom is to ensure our students are successful learners, and we simply cannot do that if we are not checking what they know—all of them—on a daily basis.

A final note about formative assessments and the process of checking student understandings. Too often in today's educational speak, school administrators and leaders are inadvertently over-complicating the idea behind formative assessment. Teachers are asked to bring back data on formative assessments (which we will cover in depth in Chapter 5), and the pressure to collect a score can create an inaccurate definition of what a formative truly is.

Formative means to inform—plain and simple. A formative does not have to be (though it could be) a quiz or contain multiple choice questions. Depending on your summative assessment, you may *want* a few formatives to make a more test-like format, but we should not simply replace the term quiz with formative. We have personally seen far too many quizzes that did not drive instruction, and they in turn were not formative assessments. The two ideas are not synonymous, and we think this is an incredibly important distinction for instructional leaders and teachers.

What's the most important aspect of a formative assessment? The questions asked of each and every student. It's important to realize that the questions you ask in a formative need to match the rigor of the questions on the summative assessment. A student cannot "level up," so to speak, from a formative to the summative. That means that if your formative assesses a lower-level question, but the summative assesses the skill at a higher level, the students cannot make that transition. Students can level down, but not up.

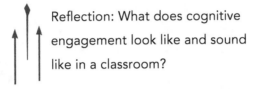

Reflection: What does cognitive engagement look like and sound like in a classroom?

Chapter 5:

# The Four Bases of PLC

"It's more important than ever that educators
collaborate to continually improve and
support the success of each learner."

– Dr. Gene Carter

IN 2019, WHEN WE STARTED the process of writing this
book, nearly 100 different school districts had come to visit
Brownsburg—most with the specific request to observe and learn
about its PLC structures. Brownsburg welcomes leaders and visitors from all districts and openly shares the intimate details of its
systems. The leaders and teachers in Brownsburg believe in equity
and accessibility, and they also believe in their PLC process. In a
sense, the entire corporation is its own professional learning community. Leaders and teachers welcome the opportunity to teach
and support other schools in their journeys with PLCs.

Richard DuFour, successful school leader and author of the
book *Professional Learning Communities at Work: Best Practices for
Enhancing Student Achievement,* is responsible for the development of these core questions that should guide each PLC meet-

ing. Much of the PLC structure we will detail in this chapter is directly or loosely based off of the work of DuFour and his staff at Adlai Stevenson High School in Lincolnshire, Illinois.

1.  **What do we want our students to know?**
2.  **How will we know they learned it?**
3.  **How will we respond if they struggle?**
4.  **How will we respond if they show mastery?**

As we unpack these questions, we ask that you continually reflect on the directness of each. Neither DuFour's team nor ours suggests that you reinvent the wheel in terms of meeting expectations or discussion protocols. These four questions are simply stated and powerful tools for creating actionable change in instruction and school environments. They are student-centered, and they repeat. Every. Single. Week.

The four questions guide instructional decisions on the micro level each week as groups of teachers analyze meaningful data to determine best instructional practices. But, we have also found that these four questions, said differently, should also drive macro-level curriculum and assessment development at a grade, building, or district level. When schools and districts truly embrace the constancy of these four questions—and they keep both these questions (and the time allotted to answer them each week) sacred—that's when the shift truly begins to take shape.

Let's look at the questions side by side, at the micro and macro levels, in Table 5.1.

Table 5.1 Micro vs. Macro Levels

| Micro: | Macro: |
|---|---|
| What do we want our students to know? | Curriculum |
| How will we know they learned it? | Assessments |
| How will we respond if they struggle? | Intervention |
| How will we respond if they show mastery? | Enrichment |

In a very clear sense, the entire mantra of *Tight-Loose-Tight* should be played out each week in the conversations with these four guiding questions. What do we want students to know? That's the narrowed, standards-based curriculum. How will we know they have learned it? Which **formative** or **summative assessments** are we giving this week to check their understanding? How will we respond to struggle and mastery? That of course is the Loose, the art, the craft of teaching.

Another important note about how *Tight-Loose-Tight* is present and relevant at PLC meetings: this is the barometer, the third point, the gauge on which many decisions will be made during discussions. A third point is a useful concept to consider when leading meetings, particularly discussion regarding data. If you can train your leaders (and members) to view curriculum, data, and documents as facts—third points aside from the members of the team at the table—then the conversation becomes less personal. Rather than leaders directing pointed questions at their peers about why some results are higher or lower, everyone can look at the data on paper—the third point—to recognize what it is telling us. Normalizing the idea of third points in conversations is a simple, highly effective strategy that equips teams with tools to focus on information over emotion as they process through the four questions. One excellent resource we recommend regarding effective protocols is *Leading Impact Teams.*

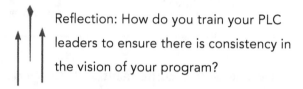

Reflection: How do you train your PLC leaders to ensure there is consistency in the vision of your program?

## Question 1: What Do We Want Our Students to Know?

Have you ever sat in a meeting where the purpose was murky at best? There was no agenda, no clear start and end time, no clear leader even? On top of that, you weren't exactly sure what your outcomes or action steps should be when the meeting ended (whenever that may be). Recall how you felt (or feel) in meetings like this. Were you productive, focused, and ready to act? Or were you confused, frustrated, and bogged down by the lack of clarity—lost in the changing details?

To have a productive PLC process, teachers must have a solid, clear path to follow in terms of curriculum. Can you begin your PLC process in a school or district without a narrowed, well-developed curriculum? Cautiously we say yes—but only because we have worked with far too many schools who have chosen this path and are struggling to live it. Can you do it? Oh, it can be attempted and fought through. Is it the best way? Absolutely not.

The aligned, standards-based curriculum is the essential first step to creating a successful PLC environment in your schools. When the curriculum is laid out, there is clarity. Teachers know that to answer the first question of PLC—"What do we want our students to know?"—they simply need to look at the already clarified curriculum map. There they should find the most important standard and objective for the week, and that question is over and done with. Simple. Once they have the "What" question answered, they can move on to the important discussions about assessment, intervention, and enrichment. If they do not have the "What" question answered, they will sit there, spinning into an unproductive, possibly frustrating meeting that fails to accomplish its goals.

Part of our responsibilities as curriculum administrators has been to coach and guide PLCs in our district. We can attest to the fact that when you ask a group of teachers to accomplish a task, the overwhelming majority honestly wants to do so. Teachers are fantastic people who typically aim to please. They are hardworking and they constantly request more time to collaborate with one another to learn and grow.

So why are so many PLC systems failing our teachers?

There is a fundamental lack of clarity in curriculum in far too many schools across our country.

When we present on PLC development, we use a baseball analogy to explain the micro/macro steps. Each step is a base, and we stress the importance of beginning at first base every time. You cannot simply skip first when you're playing ball, and likewise you cannot skip the first step (curriculum development) when creating PLCs. Still, that is exactly what so many schools try to do.

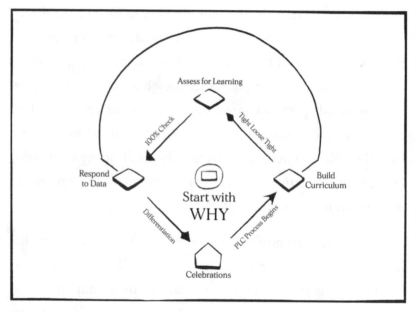

**Figure 5.1** The Macro Level View of PLC Process

When PLCs do not have a guaranteed, viable curriculum guiding their progress, valuable time is wasted in this first question. Groups can take entire meetings attempting to decide what should be taught and why. If PLC members are not paced closely, within days of one another, the conversation of what to teach next becomes cumbersome and in some cases impossible.

No one wants to back track on a skill they've already covered and assessed, and no one wants to feel rushed to "catch up" to the rest of the team—especially not for the sake of data reporting. Few things frustrate a teacher more than being asked to complete a task that feels arbitrary and meaningless. Without a clear, easy-to-follow curriculum, teachers spin their wheels trying to decide on common assessments for the sake of appeasement and compliance. Again, teachers tend to be pleasers, and they do what is asked of them. That does not mean they buy-in, nor does it mean they see the value of giving random assessments to analyze data.

If the assessment is void of importance, it will never truly be used to impact learning for students. School administrators need to coach their PLC leaders (and yes, each PLC needs a designated leader) to ensure that assessments are truly valuable and covering important material. There is no point in bringing data back on a quiz if the plan is to move on from that quiz regardless of the outcome. Why would anyone want to discuss data that has come and gone and makes no impact on their classroom?

You get the point. In order to prevent these types of superficial, obligatory conversations from becoming the norm in the PLC process, you must fight to establish solid curriculum and pacing in each of your subject areas. The process for developing curriculum can take upwards of two years if done with fidelity. Include checkpoints and opportunities for curriculum teams to receive feedback on their decisions. And remember: curriculum development is truly an ongoing, continuous process. You will never be "done" with curriculum revisions or alignment. Normalize your teams to believe that revision is part of the strength of the process.

Teachers are the ones closest to implementing the curriculum, so they should have a strong stake in the development of what they will teach. If your district currently uses prescribed programs for curriculum, we strongly encourage you to re-evaluate their effectiveness. Reading, writing, and math series are far more effective for broad use at the elementary level than the secondary level. The main reason: your goal should be to teach the standards, not to cover the material provided in your textbook. Very rarely does a textbook (or online learning tool) actually address the most critical standards. If teachers blindly follow the book, there is little to no room for a focus on critical standards.

It can be difficult to guide teachers through the process of curriculum development, but the buy-in is worth it. Use your professional development money to keep your teachers in house; bring in experts (or find experts in your district) who can guide these conversations. Don't feel like you need to get into the weeds in curriculum design—you just need to help teachers establish the main standards they will focus on, and why. We recommend forgoing conversations about agreed-upon learning activities or vocabulary at first. You want to get the standards, objectives, and assessments paced, and eventually the other pieces can come—if the teachers say so.

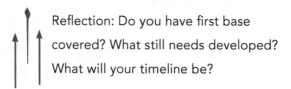

Reflection: Do you have first base covered? What still needs developed? What will your timeline be?

## Question 2: How Will We Know They've Learned It?

Teaching is an art, and we truly believe that you are called into this profession to make a difference in the lives of others. The best teachers, the ones who light the fires and fan the flames, understand that it's not about what they taught—it's about what their students learned. Teaching a lesson that no one understands is a great way to fuel your ego, but it isn't exactly the best way to improve society, make an impact, or keep your job. More and more of today's teachers are leaving their university or transition programs prepared to teach for all learners—and we are excited to be active in this paradigm shift in education.

The second question of the PLC cycle is all about checking for understanding of your students' learning: Do they really understand the concept? How do I know for sure? Teachers who ask themselves these questions continually, throughout their lessons (not just at the end) are the most highly effective educators in the field. This portion of the PLC cycle is there to allow teachers the space to brainstorm and create purposeful checks for understanding in the midst of their most complicated lessons. It's important to teach your teachers—possibly every year—that assessment is all about what the students know at that given moment. Once I know what they know, I can then decide my next instructional steps. If I assume what they know, I'm not truly meeting their needs. If I find out what they know and ignore the results, I'm not truly meeting their needs. I must determine the best way to check, and then, do something with the information.

Assessment is a big word, and we fear it could become a catchphrase far too soon. Which is ridiculous if you think about it because assessing learning is a cornerstone of any part of every educational experience. Even if you are teaching yourself photography or gardening, you still assess your progress and determine next steps. Assessment has been, and always will be, needed. But, what do you do with the data? Well, that's where we could all use a bit more consistency.

## Formative vs. Summative Assessment

Data can be broken into more than two types of categories, but for all intents and purposes, we are going to nutshell the difference between formative and summative assessments.

On the macro level, summative assessments need to be created or selected after the curriculum alignment work is completed. Summatives are the summation; they assess what was learned or attained at the end of a unit. Summatives might include tests, essays, projects, portfolios, speeches, as well as state and national assessments. Typically, a summative signals the end of one unit of study and the transition into the next unit. Though skills may cycle and repeat from unit to unit, a summative is truly the benchmark and end.

On the micro level, PLCs do need to review summative assessment data at key moments throughout the year. We recommend that teachers begin the year with some type of data roster that details previous years' summative assessment information. The roster might include state assessment results, credits attained,

SAT/ACT scores, AP or dual-credit work, as well as varying support designations (such as ILPs, IEPs, and 504s). Teachers should have this information at the start of their year (or semester) so that they can determine which students need more support and in which areas. The summative data from prior years does not necessarily determine the current year's achievement, but it can provide teachers with at least a starting point for each student.

As formal summative pieces are gathered throughout the year, teachers should review this data in their PLC teams. Summative assessments should be written before units are taught, as they are the end goal for each unit or course. Too often, PLCs are caught in the trap of writing their assessments as they teach their curriculum, and that will simply never work. Summative assessments should be identical, meaning if there are four biology teachers, then all four should give the exact same version of the assessment at the end of the unit. Mr. Jones is not allowed to add his favorite 10 questions that are outside of the agreed-upon curriculum. Mrs. Murphy is not allowed to cut questions 12–14 because her class ran out of time and she had to cut a lesson mid-unit. Every teacher should be held accountable for teaching the narrowed, standards-based curriculum in the agreed-upon time frame. Then, the identical summative assessment should be given.

Writing questions for assessments is difficult work, and often it pushes teachers to grow in professional ways they had never before considered. It is important to note that quality assessments consider the depth of knowledge of the standards they address. Students cannot level up in terms of depth of knowledge (resource on page D1 of the Appendix), so teachers must be purposeful in the questions they use to teach and the questions they use on assessments. For example, it's inappropriate to ask students to think in terms of identification during lessons, but then assess them on their ability to analyze that same concept. If you're going to assess a skill at a certain depth of knowledge, you must teach that skill at the same depth.

This is not control for control sake, nor is it a way to simply frustrate veteran teachers who have taught their content for the past however many years without interruption. This is the face of equity; it's a common, viable curriculum.

When students (and parents) know that all 10th graders taking geometry will have the same common exam at the end of a unit, there is an elimination of competition or favoritism in regard to teachers. From a collegial standpoint, school culture is strengthened as all staff know they are equally accountable for providing a common curriculum for all students. The English teachers don't have to worry about whether or not science is given common assessments—they are! Second grade no longer questions what's happening in first grade—they can look and see. Weak teachers cannot hide, nor can rock stars. This is a system that celebrates collaboration, commitment, and equity. It is about student learning, not teacher egos. A true professional learning community is a community where all members show up and follow-through. This is not a space where teachers can say one thing to their group, then do another in the safety of their classrooms. Accountability breeds excellence for all.

## Formative Assessment

If summative assessments are the ending destination, then formative assessments are the highway signs and checkpoints along the way. Formative means *to inform*, and this type of data is truly the bread and butter of PLC. Formative assessments should happen daily, and in the best classrooms they do. Questioning, discussion, checking for understanding—this is what education is all about. More and more practitioners are entering the field of education with a desire to ensure learning for the student—not simply to display their content prowess. This essential paradigm shift in education is the cornerstone behind quality instruction. As more and more teachers seek to create learning environments for *all students*, success and achievement will continue to rise.

At the macro level, common formative assessments can occur among groups of teachers when they have a narrow curriculum that is easily followed by all. If it seems we're beating a dead horse here, you are absolutely right. With a common curriculum, teachers can do the meaningful work of digging into standards, processing misconceptions, and finally creating checks for understanding that provide them with data they will actually use. Without the common map, teachers will spin their wheels hemming and hawing about potential skills to assess. Too often, the easy assessment to create is chosen as the common formative— not because of its instructional impact, but because it allows the teachers to settle on a decision. Teachers are pleasers, and they want to meet expectations set by their leaders. If asked to determine a common assessment with their peers, they will do so even if the assessment lacks purpose and instructional impact.

We do not fault the teachers for this; the fault lies entirely with their school leaders for failing to provide them the clarity of curriculum needed to have meaningful discussions about data.

Here is another example of how the formative assessment trap plays out in far too many PLCs:

> Mr. Warner's PLC just had a productive meeting, and they are walking away with a sense of accomplishment. Unlike last week, when they couldn't agree upon a common assessment, this week they all agreed to use the Chapter 2 quiz he created in preparation for the meeting. The quiz has 15 questions, and all are written at the appropriate depth of knowledge for the standards. At the time of their meeting, they were two days into the chapter and were able to discuss struggles they'd witnessed among their students. They all agreed to give the common quiz on Friday, and they will bring their data back next week when they meet again. Below is a timeline of their lesson plans:

Table 5.2 Sample Weekly Plan

| Tues. | Wed. | Thurs. | Fri. | Mon. |
|-------|------|--------|------|------|
| Day 1 Chp 2 | Day 2 Chp 2 | Day 3 Chp 2 | Quiz Chp 2 | Day 1 Chp 3 |

From the outside, this looks like a solid PLC meeting for all of the reasons detailed above. The issue? The formative is actually a summative, and the teachers don't even know it.

How can that be? They are giving a quiz (that leads up to the larger test—the summative) and this is a checkpoint, not the end assessment. That makes it a formative, right?

Almost, but not quite.

The entire purpose of a formative is to drive instruction. The problem here is not the formative itself; the problem is how the teachers are viewing the quiz in terms of their unit design. The issue is Monday. They move on to the next chapter without building in a day for differentiation, intervention, or extension. What was the point of giving the assessment on Friday if the plan was to move forward regardless of the information provided from the quiz? If you aren't going to use the data, don't gather it.

Here's another option: take the 15 questions on the quiz and break them up over the four days of instruction for the chapter. Assess the students' understanding each day, and take one of those short, four or five question checks and bring those results back for data. With your PLC, determine how to re-teach that particular element of the chapter, or create a differentiated lesson where students work through the specific struggle area that *they* face before moving on.

When you treat a formative like a summative, there is pressure to perform. Teachers believe the data are more about their effectiveness than what the students need to learn next. This is counter-productive to creating an open, supportive learning community. Teachers need to view one another as allies, and purposeful conversation and training about formative data is paramount if school leaders want to foster authentic learning communities with their teachers.

> Reflection: Now that you have first base covered, what about second? Are common summatives developed and in place? What training does your staff need in this area?

## Question 3: How Will We Respond If They Struggle?

The entire purpose of gathering data and discussing it in teams is to decide upon action steps that will best meet the varying learning needs of students. Questions 3 and 4 ideally go together in the PLC process, but we'll break them down separately for clarity's sake.

Once a team has identified the students who struggled with a particular skill, the next step in the PLC process is to determine what they will do for those students. Differentiation is a flashy term that has erupted across the education landscape over the past decade, but differentiation doesn't have to be frightening or fear-invoking. If a team can determine who needs what re-taught, then differentiation can take place.

In a high-functioning PLC, the team believes in the power of data—not for data sake—but because the information shows which students need which intervention, small group, re-teach, level, and so on. When a culture of growth is established, teachers want to share their results and rely on one another for ideas on how to improve. They are comfortable enough to take risks together, and they most definitely reap the rewards together, too.

There are entire books written about the benefits of data impacting instruction, but it's incredibly easy for groups to miss the boat when deciding how to use data in meetings. Too often, teams believe they are meeting expectations by simply bringing back averages or scores, when in reality the scores are not used to impact decision-making.

For example, if the seventh-grade English PLC brings back overall average scores on a 4-question formative assessment—how can they use this data? What does the average tell each teacher about which students need what support? They can see how well groups of students performed in comparison to other groups of students, but what more? With overall averages, it's also tempting for teachers to defend, shift, and hide as they also feel on display with their scores. There is an unintended creation of comparison between the teachers, and one that really should be avoided whenever possible.

But what if this same group of teachers agrees to bring back the names of students who didn't pass the assessment? How much more useful is this data? Now, instead of looking at an overall average that does little to impact their teaching, they can look at the names of actual students to determine who might need extra support. And let's be clear: extra support does not have to be complicated, ornate, or require a change of schedule or additional staffing—some of the time, yes, but most of the time, no. Extra support often comes in the form of simply more time with the teacher, in one-on-one or small groups, or with timely feedback (or Tier 1 supports). The PLC might take a look at this group of names and decide that the very next day, all of the students who struggled will be grouped together during a certain activity so that the teacher can provide more feedback and support. Or, the PLC might agree that they'll substitute Friday's bell work with another practice for these students who struggled. Maybe they'll create a station activity or find leveled reading passages. Maybe they'll find ways to integrate more choice and personal connection into upcoming lessons to better draw in their struggling learners. Or maybe they will make it a point to call on the struggling students more—not less—to keep engagement high and checks for understanding frequent. Regardless of what they decide, a high-functioning PLC makes the decisions as a team.

When data is about who needs what, teachers buy in. They get this concept because it's essentially the heart of all teaching. We are all in this business, we hope, to help figure out the answers to who needs what. This is the great riddle of education, and as leaders, we need to help our teachers embrace the riddle week after week, year after year. We don't get into education to find the next new "thing" each week. We get into education to help students learn what they don't know. And we certainly do not get into education to teach students what they know already.

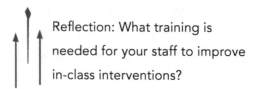

Reflection: What training is needed for your staff to improve in-class interventions?

## Question 4: How will we respond if they show mastery?

Have you ever been to a conference and left mid-presentation because you already knew the material? Ever started a book and quit after a few chapters because you were bored or knew the information? Have you ever worked with a colleague or leader who did not assume your competence? If you answered "No" to any of these questions, you're either nicer than us or not exactly telling the truth. Either way, this feeling of complacency, boredom, and presumed incompetency is unfortunately running rampant among many of today's youth.

If half of the reason we look at data after an assessment is to determine intervention needs for the strugglers, then the other half of the reason is to also determine the needs of the students who don't need extra support. Call it extension, enrichment, acceleration, or more—we just call this good, responsive teaching. Few things are worse for a student than to hear they showed mastery of a skill, but will go ahead and do more practice on it anyways because other classmates need the extra support. Think about it: why are we collecting data on student progress if we aren't going to allow them to truly progress? Why did I need to know they were ready to move on if I'm not going to let them move on? What is the point of this data?

We once worked with a PLC who had a 100-question pretest that they gave at the beginning of the year. This pretest covered the concepts that would be covered throughout the course, many of which were repeat skills from previous years (but that's a different conversation). In one of their first meetings of the year, the

PLC of four teachers was sharing their overall averages (again, for what purpose?) and then pinpointing a few trouble areas where students struggle (okay, better).

Overwhelmingly, the students aced certain parts of the pre-test and then struggled in other areas. They were able to identify three main areas of grammar where overall the students struggled, but when pressed to explain how this data were going to impact their instruction, their responses sounded something like this, "Well, we review infinitive phrases in November" and "Yes, students always tend to struggle with commas." In other words, they would "address" the concerns in their already planned curriculum. Kudos to this group for having their Tight-Loose-Tight curriculum determined, but the problem with their approach was that they gave a huge assessment that could not be used effectively to actually influence instruction. Which students struggled with commas in August, and how would that information impact comma instruction in December? No clue. And what about the students who earned an 80% or higher on that pretest? Did they get to earn an automatic credit for the course since they proved in week one that they already had mastery of the concepts?

At one point in our district, many teachers and PLCs were instructed by coaches and SDHs to create pre-assessments with the intention that these assessments would help teachers determine appropriate steps in their units. The problem with monster pre-assessments is that the valuable information can get lost in the sheer volume of questions or coverage of content. If you're going to give a pre-assessment, make it small and manageable—for each unit or chapter—rather than for an entire quarter or semester. Be sure to organize the assessment by skill and common misconceptions to help you determine which skills are weaknesses for which students, and then be prepared to provide more challenging work for students who are able to show, "I already know this" on Day 1.

Question 4 should be answered each week, yes, but it must also be answered on a larger scale, and PLCs need to know this, especially if pre-assessments are being used. We once had a dual-credit teacher give a pre-assessment to seniors. The students averaged a 94% on this assessment and the teacher was excited to have "good" data. When asked how the data was actually going to influence instruction, the teacher merely blinked. Needless to say, she wasn't too happy when we told her the data was concerning to us. If a group of students can average a 94% on a pretest, then the material is far too easy. That type of data is alarming to say the least. But how many teachers would realize this without leadership helping them to see that "good" data isn't necessarily high? We believe the number to be low.

Teachers need to feel empowered to work in collaborative teams to push the curriculum for students who need the challenge. This might not mean acceleration, per se, but it should include higher levels of questions (think Bloom's Taxonomy and depth of knowledge), more creativity, and choice.

Differentiation is not a soft skill idea for teachers in younger grade levels; it's especially important that teachers of older students utilize differentiation as well. When students begin to realize their strengths and interests, they need to be supported by teachers who will continue to provide feedback, choice, and challenge to support them in their growth. High school students in particular need teachers who are willing to let them explore and challenge themselves with innovation and enrichment. Allowing students to pursue passion projects or real-world connections to content is one of the most influential strategies to engaging older learners. Teens are searching for relevance and meaning in all things—but especially high school geometry, chemistry, and French II. When we can recognize when certain students are in need of a challenge or more creative opportunities, we draw them in to their learning. They own their progress and become invested in the course. This is not an easy task to accomplish, but it's needed and it's possible.

The conversation around Question 4 should ideally happen before a unit begins, and then each week while teachers are deciding how to respond to struggling students. Essentially, they should think of this part of the PLC like this: What lesson (or part of the lesson) are we going to differentiate for our students? When we're working with our strugglers, what do our non-strugglers need to do? Why?

In other words, this is lesson design. Or question design. Or grouping design. Whatever the PLC decides. Who needs what and when? That's what PLC is all about. The four questions—the four bases—help determine the answer to this question each week. They keep the wheels on the bus and the curriculum moving forward without disregarding the needs of students' each week.

 Reflection: What training is needed for staff on enrichment? Differentiation? When you think of your current system for teacher growth and professional learning communities, which base are you on?

# Chapter 6:

# Structures of a PLC

"Greatness is not a function of circumstance.
Greatness, it turns out, is largely a matter of
conscious choice, and discipline."

– Jim Collins, *Good to Great*

## Protocols, Protocols, Protocols

ASIDE FROM THE FOUR ESSENTIAL questions, highly effective
PLCs need predictable structures and expectations for the group
to thrive. Providing time for a meeting to occur is not the same
as planning a meeting, and teachers have enough to plan as is.
Leaders need to help carry the load of this planning by creating expectations and protocols—systems—that all PLC members
are required to follow. Yes, PLCs should cycle through the four
essential questions each week—but there's more to the story if
you want the meetings to truly promote growth for teachers and
students.

The first protocol that we cannot emphasize enough is the need
to require **all of your teachers to meet together in a common space.**

If you provide PLC time every Wednesday morning for 30 minutes before school, ask your teachers to meet in the media center. They will still sit with their small teams, but meeting in the common space will instill a shared belief in the common vision behind PLCs. Don't have a common PLC time for your entire staff? Ask your teachers to meet, staggered throughout the day, in a common space. For example, you might have your teams meet during staggered prep periods. Whoever is supposed to PLC during second-period prep on Tuesday—those teachers should meet in a common area. Again, there is power in getting teachers physically into a new, common space that is dedicated to group learning and decision-making. It is far too easy and comfortable to rest on our laurels when we meet with colleagues in our typical classroom walls.

Think your teachers will easily buy in to this simple proximity shift? We caution you to think again. Be prepared for questions and skepticism from your teachers if you do not do enough of the yeoman's work required to explain your rationale behind meeting as a large team. Clarify over and over again that meeting together is not about micromanagement or "spying" on PLC work; it's about shared accountability, access to coaches and administrators, and a common, visible vision.

The second protocol that is a must (and will also create potential questioning from your staff) is to require **every PLC to keep an agenda and notes of each meeting each week**. An example agenda can be found on page B3 of the Appendix. Administrators or coaches can physically create the agendas or PLC leaders can be responsible for this task themselves, but essentially each group will record the following information:

➡ **Celebrations**
➡ **Data from previous week**
➡ **Response to data**
➡ **Cycle through four essential questions**

Some schools and organizations require notes, but there is no follow-up or feedback provided to the groups. Without the feedback, individual PLCs are left to wonder: *Is anyone even reading this? Are all the other PLCs actually filling this out? What's the point? Don't they trust me as a professional? What are we doing wrong?*

If you claim to believe in the power of feedback in your school, then you need to practice what you preach. **Providing feedback to PLCs each week is a quick, productive way for building leaders to catch snapshots of curriculum at work.** Feedback also works to create the culture that we're all capable of growing and learning from one another. Data analysis is monitored (not for the results but for the quality of discussion around the results) and stagnation is avoided.

Is all feedback equal? Absolutely not. In fact, we offer a word of caution for all administrators, coaches, and leaders who provide the needed feedback each week: look for the positives and reinforce the behaviors you wish to see. When a PLC seems to misunderstand a portion of an agenda or completely ignores specific items week after week, consider the various ways to approach the team to discuss the concerns in person. Grilling a group of teachers each week with questions can feel intimidating, and that will actually create the opposite atmosphere you're hoping to establish in your building.

On the other hand, if you can position yourself and your team as instructional leaders who believe in the power of adult learning and growth, then meaningful feedback and conversations will nudge and pull your groups along. Leaders must be humble and relational in the feedback they provide, and they should consider providing feedback on both the content and the facilitation of the meeting.

Which brings us to another protocol: **normalize the practice of visitors who attend PLC meetings.** If you truly believe that PLCs are real, professional development, then you need to physically show up to the meetings ready to listen and support. Principals, assistant principals, curriculum directors, special education leaders, data analysts, and instructional coaches should all make it a point to visit PLCs across the district. When the leaders sit at the table, focus, and engage, the teachers believe the conversation is important. Principals should be prepared to again clarify the *why* behind these visits (no, they are not listening in to spy or "catch" teachers making mistakes). Rather, they are there to gain snippets of information, to keep an accurate pulse of the status of PLCs and their effectiveness overall. In a sense, participating in these meetings provides leaders with formative data on the progress of PLCs in their department, school, and district. So, be present at these meetings. Put your phone away. Unplug from whatever happened during the day—which we know, is a lot. Reply to the email later. Sit, be present, and listen.

When beginning your PLC process each year, make it a point to call teachers to create their own protocols or norms for their meetings. An example of how we develop our PLC Norms is on page F1 of the Appendix. Some groups know they are chattier and more apt to get off-topic. Other groups share that they are quick to avoid rigorous discourse if they fear hurting each other's feelings. As the leader, create a protocol that **requires PLCs to create meaningful norms each year**, and then, train the PLC members to distinguish purposeful norms from ones that look nice on paper.

There are other details to consider when organizing PLCs in your school. If you work in an elementary setting, consider the various content areas that your teachers should cycle through every month. What are your must-haves? We recommend planning for at least one math, one reading, and one writing week a month. The fourth week might be open for science/social studies or provide a flex week for teachers to dive further into summative data (if relevant).

What do your related arts teachers need? What if you only have one music teacher and one art teacher? What about world languages? AP courses? Small schools in general? What do you do when you only have a PLC of one?

This is a question we've gotten consistently through the years, and our advice is to have common discipline teachers meet together when possible. For example, if you have three related arts teachers in your building, but they each teach a different subject, that team can still meet to discuss best practice, data from their own content, and student-centered interventions.

The same for three AP world language teachers. The AP French, Spanish, and German teachers might all teach different courses, but they can relate in terms of the issues their students face, and they can share strategies that will benefit each other.

What if you only have one sixth-grade English teacher, one seventh-grade English teacher, and one eighth-grade English teacher? We recommend that this group should meet each week and follow the same four questions. It might be that they're each teaching a different novel or having students respond to different writing pieces, but the overall skills could be aligned and cycled in a similar fashion. Vertical articulation happens when grade levels and content areas overlap in purposeful discussion. These situations are opportunities for alignment not obstacles to overcome.

Special education staff, counselors, and social workers are other groups to consider when planning your PLC rotations. How do the needs of these teams vary from the traditional grade-level teams? What protocols should remain consistent, and what questions need to change?

Ultimately, protocols create a sense of common expectations across a building (or district) and these protocols help to establish and maintain the belief that PLCs are vital to the work of your teachers.

One final suggestion that we offer to visiting school districts is to arrange for an annual PLC leadership training, or summit, to support and coach your leaders in this process. PLC leaders often change from year to year, and it's important that all leaders feel equipped to meet the expectations set by the district or school. When expectations are assumed, they are murky and often unmet. When teachers are trained and supported each year, expectations are clarified, monitored, and reinforced. The ongoing training also reiterates the belief that the PLC process is important and vital to the success of both staff and students. A yearly leadership summit is an outward proclamation that the work of PLCs is a core tenet of the district's vision.

Utilize your administrative team or skilled teacher-leaders to organize and host the summit, and use professional development money to pay PLC leaders stipends for attending. Honor their time, and you honor their work.

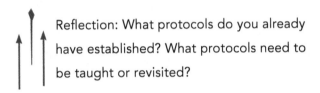

Reflection: What protocols do you already have established? What protocols need to be taught or revisited?

# Chapter 7:
# Supports for Teachers

"Don't wait until you reach your goal
to be proud of yourself. Be proud
of every step you take."

– Karen Salmansohn

## What Every Teacher Wants to Know

ONE OF OUR FAVORITE ASPECTS of our curriculum leadership roles is that we are responsible for hiring most, if not all, of the teachers in our departments. If you empower the people closest to the decisions to make the decisions, growth happens. We always save the final few moments of an interview for questions from our candidates, and there is one common question that is asked nearly 100% of the time:

*How will I be supported here?*

Recent graduates who've just wrapped up student teaching placements are especially anxious to hear how they will be supported, and perhaps surprisingly so are veterans. But, why shouldn't they be? Teaching is one of the most rewarding *and demanding* professions that exist in our society, and it isn't exactly touted as one of prestige, stability, and unwavering respect. The days are long; the needs are high; the expectations are intense. Stress in many schools is visceral, felt by teachers, students, parents, and all staff alike. When a threatening culture is alive in a school, it's difficult to feel safe. If you don't feel safe, you won't take risks. This goes for both teachers and students. Honestly, it goes for the leadership, as well.

**And highly effective instruction must be inclusive of risk.**

Hiring great teachers, especially ones fresh out of their teaching programs, is no easy task. More and more throughout the years we have realized the importance of both parties finding each other to be the "right fit." A large part of what we're looking for in our screening interviews and model lessons is whether or not we see these new teachers as future teammates of our current teachers. After our quick introductions about why they want to teach with us, and after we've asked a few teaching-based questions, we dive into questions that we hope will show us who we're really talking to. We ask questions like, "What do you do when you feel overwhelmed? How do you relieve stress? What do you do for fun? What are you the most passionate about in life? How do you need to be supported?"

After the initial screening interview, the next step is a model lesson round. To make it to this round, we are looking for a few key characteristics. If a candidate conveys sincerity, humility, and reflection, we typically see them as someone we can work with.

If a candidate offers stock answers, or says they never really get stressed out, we quickly realize that they might be a wonderful teacher one day . . . they just won't be a teacher with us. Because the reality is everyone gets stressed out from time to time; that's life when you are pushing your limits. Part of what our new teachers need to learn—especially in our current educational climate—is that one of their biggest jobs starting out is to embrace the fact that they will feel stressed, they will feel overwhelmed, they will feel utterly defeated at times.

They need to see—right from the start—that they are about to enter into the most rewarding and exhausting profession, and in order to excel in this field, they will often push themselves to their limits. The key for people like us (you know, the ones who get the awesome responsibility of offering our new, energized, and excited teachers their "first shot") is to do everything we can to keep these teachers from falling over the edge.

If a leader's first responsibility to a new teacher is to make sure we have set them up in the right school and system, that they truly has found a good "match" in us, then our second responsibility is to do everything we can to earn their trust. It is imperative that new teachers feel absolute trust from their administrators—especially from the person who hired them. Beginning a new career can often be a frightening experience. New teachers are trying to learn their school system, the hidden norms of their building, colleagues' names, how to find the printer, and of course what to teach. They are often worried sick that they will look foolish in front of their students, peers, and administrators. They are nervous about their abilities to put philosophy into action. They are judging themselves, and they often worry about the judgment they will receive from their evaluator. But that's not all they worry about.

Our new teachers today are also worried that no one will push them to grow. They worry they won't get the much sought-after feedback they crave, and they are worried they will be abandoned to all their own devices. They aren't worried that they will be told what to do—they are worried that no one will tell them what to do. New teachers worry that they don't know the most effective practices to reach their students, and they worry that no one will ever step in to help them figure it out. They worry they are secret frauds. They worry that they are secret rock stars—hidden behind stacks of assessments to grade.

Worry and anxiety are heavy burdens to carry. They weigh on our new teachers, and they push them closer to that proverbial edge. It is my responsibility to my new teachers to earn their trust—and quickly—so that they can drop some of these weights and put more energy into creating engaging lessons for their students. So, how do leaders do this?

## Be a Coach

First and foremost, teachers need a coach who understands the intricacies of their position and student level. Instructional coaches are vitally important aspects of thriving school cultures, and in Brownsburg are often selected by peers as Teacher of the Year in elementary buildings. In this district, an instructional coach is housed at each of the seven elementary schools and secondary department heads (SDHs) lead the 6–12 core departments, including English, math, science, social studies, special education, and world language. The instructional coaches and SDHs serve as the coaches throughout the district, but assistant principals, principals, and building directors are also viewed as influential instructional leaders. The coaches work alongside the building leaders to support all teachers in various ways.

Aside from the day-to-day building-level supports that teachers receive from their administrators, their coaches provide the ongoing instructional support that helps to create the safe, risk-taking enabled environment that leads to student and teacher success. In the beginning, coaches and SDHs are responsible for onboarding new hires and making expectations clear and attainable. We recommend that district leaders agree (if they've not done this already) to use the same evaluation tools across the district, and incorporate teaching discussions around the evaluation tool from the beginning. When teachers know what is expected of them from the start, they are more likely to meet said expectations. Honestly, this is true of most individuals, regardless of the career field.

New teachers need to view their administrators as their coach, not their boss. Here's the reality: they know you're their boss. This automatically creates distance and the slightest of slight tension between you. Not all tension is bad; in fact, certain amounts of tension and stress are thought to increase our abilities to perform at high levels. The fact remains, however, that it's a leader's job to help this new teacher grow, and they will only do this if they view you as a trusted, invested coach who wants them to succeed. Coaches support. Coaches push their players to work hard, reach new limits, and attain new goals. Shouldn't we do the same for our teachers?

When we describe our administrative role to new teachers, the first responsibility that we share is that we are coaches. It is our priority to listen, to get to know them, to earn their trust. And leaders need their teachers to know them, as well. Administrators need to be human and humble. We need to talk about our own interests, families, triumphs, and failures. We need to openly share our growth areas and describe our own journeys through education. Regardless of how many years you have invested in education, your new teachers need to see and hear you as the first-year-teacher version of yourself, too. We have all been there. We all had to start somewhere. We have all struggled.

## Be a Cheerleader

New teachers are going to make mistakes. They will not be perfect, and they know this. What they don't know is how amazing they are. They don't see their energy and spirit. They don't see how their students light up when they enter the room. They don't realize how hard they are working. Part of effectively coaching teachers means that we need to build up their confidence.

We are not suggesting that you fill their heads with alternate realities about their instruction or management, but you do need to encourage them. We need our teachers to be willing to take risks. These highly effective strategies that they are craving to learn . . . well, to a new teacher, this is a risk. We need the teaching environment in a school culture to be safe and secure. You need your new teachers to trust that you know they will mess up (psst, you knew that when you hired them).

Leaders should be there to try to help them avoid these pitfalls as much as possible, but when they fall they have to know we'll catch them. New teachers need to know that you will practice with them, go to bat for them, and advocate on their behalves.

## Be a Mirror

If they know they can trust their administrator, and they know their administrator wants them to succeed, then new teachers will trust the honest feedback they receive in walk-throughs and classroom visits. Per our school district expectations, we formally observe our new teachers six times a year. We know many school districts where that number is higher, and we also know districts where that number is drastically lower. We maintain that honest, relevant, timely feedback is an essential component of the trust relationship with a new teacher, therefore administrators need to get into the classroom. Even if your district only requires you to have one formal observation a year (which is hard for us to fathom), we argue that new teachers need, and—more importantly—want consistent feedback all year long. We have hired several second- and third-year teachers, and one of the shared concerns they have all expressed was the lack of consistent observational feedback they received from their former administrators.

Newer teachers want the assurance that they aren't completely messing up. They want to know what to fix—and how to do it. They also like to get a pat on the back sometimes. This isn't to say that all feedback is positive. One of the crucial components of effective feedback is knowing how to honestly deliver the tips and suggestions you have to offer. There are times when you need to be blatantly clear and say, "This needs to change," and there are times when you can take a softer approach. It's tough to be new. Want to know what's tougher? Feeling like your addition to your school was inconsequential. When we don't observe our new teachers—when we don't offer feedback for growth—our new teachers feel invisible. They feel as though they aren't worth our time. They wonder: Does anyone see me? Does anyone know how hard I'm working? Does anyone see how near the edge I am? Will anyone catch me if I do fall?

Administrators need to serve as coaching mentors if they are to gain the trust of their teaching staff. Evaluations are helpful tools that assist in creating the culture of trust . . . if used correctly. And to be honest, far too many teachers would tell us that evaluation tools are not being used correctly (for supportive growth) but rather punitively (to seemingly catch or punish teachers). Recognize that perception is reality even for your best teachers, so if your staff believes the administration is out to get them, that's a toxic culture that must be fixed as quickly as possible.

So how do you fix a distrustful culture?

➡ Come alongside your staff.
➡ Find instructional experts who can serve with you as you give tangible pieces of feedback to your teachers.

➠ Use your teachers as experts in instruction to coach and support one another.

➠ Make it a priority to lead the instructional components of your building, and surround yourself with other leaders more skilled than you in this area.

➠ Honor the person whose work you are evaluating. You are not evaluating the person; you are evaluating their work. Remember that.

When teachers feel supported—by peers, their principals, their central office—they are willing to open up their hearts and souls for learning and growth. When teachers feel supported, they are able to set aside their egos to reveal honesty, insecurities, and weak points in their instruction. When these are revealed, they are able to receive constructive feedback on how to improve—not because they believe themselves to be terrible, but because they believe in the power of growth and improvement. When you live in a positive culture that encourages collaboration and feedback, you develop a sense of true security and stability. You don't have to be perfect—you just have to be open and willing to improve. Who doesn't want to work in an environment like that?

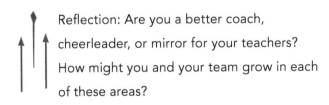

Reflection: Are you a better coach, cheerleader, or mirror for your teachers? How might you and your team grow in each of these areas?

# Chapter 8:
# Supports for Students

"I've learned that people will forget
what you said, what you did, but never
forget how you made them feel."

– Maya Angelou

STUDENTS SHOULD BE AT THE heart of all decisions that are made in a school and district. If you aren't making decisions based on the best interest of your students, you are failing as a school leader. Period.

Student-centered decisions can influence curriculum, staff, programs, and politics. Student-centered decisions keep the heart of the students, not adults, at the core of the vision. Student well-being and growth drives staffing, class sizes, budgets, and decisions in general. Student success is determined by smiles, not scores. Students know they are valued and cared for; they know they are worth fighting for; they feel a true sense of belonging and support.

Today's children come to us with more concerns and needs than is easy to imagine. Between homelessness and hunger, family battles and divorce, foster care and single-parent homes, physical and mental health, bullying, suicide, self-harm, drugs, abuse, racism, sexism, and social media, today's students are struggling. As a society, we need to recognize that today's students are tomorrow's citizens, and unless we want an anxious, unhealthy, hurting populous in our unforeseeable future, we must equip our schools to address the needs of the whole child.

When a district or school operates with clearly defined systems, it is easier to spot gaps in terms of support. If every school (or grade or class) is left to determine its own responses and protocols, critical time is wasted. Once again, there is power in expecting similar-to-identical approaches; staff and leaders become accustomed to one set of norms and approaches and they are able to get really, really good at meeting their students' needs. This same principle is applied to varying organizations, including business, hospitals, and first-responders.

## Types of Support

Because our students come to us from such a wide variety of backgrounds, it's nearly impossible to anticipate every type of need that we might encounter. Schools leaders can, however, think through many of the major areas of need and then establish clear protocols for staff. This empowers the people closest to the students to take action and meet unmet needs.

At the most basic level, school leaders need to consider both the academic and social-emotional wellness of their students. Additionally, we must provide safe and healthy learning environments every single day. We will explore each of these areas of need from the perspective of strategies that work within our system. Not all strategies are unilateral, and we recognize that there may be supports shared in this section that are irrelevant for your community. But, we do believe that the heart of supporting students is about having a plan and process, and this is regardless of the need being addressed.

We also recognize that needs for students vary by age level. Therefore, we will attempt to describe various supports in terms of both elementary approaches and secondary approaches.

## Elementary Academic Supports

After ensuring alignment with curriculum and assessments, school leaders should turn to a possibly unlikely academic support: the daily bell schedule. Consider the time students spend in various subjects, and ask yourself this question: does the schedule match our learning priorities?

For example, if you claim to value reading but do not mandate a reading block for all students, but instead allow teachers to cover chosen standards and material, then your schedule does not actually support your learning priorities. Do you believe students should be writing every day across multiple subjects? How much time is set aside, in each grade, every day, for writing?

When you stop and examine the bell schedule, the minutes are surprisingly honest.

It is shocking to see that schools within districts are allowed to create their own, unique schedules. Why does this shock us? Minutes help to monitor pacing, and pacing ensures equitable experience. Remember: we are not suggesting that differentiation *not* occur. We are, in fact, suggesting that teachers need to hold themselves accountable to providing equitable time for students to accomplish the agreed-upon outcomes within a curriculum.

Table 8.1 Sample Elementary Schedule A

| 8:00 | Arrival, Morning Meetings |
|-------|---------------------------|
| 8:15 | Language Arts/Spelling |
| 8:45 | Writing |
| 9:15 | Reading |
| 9:45 | Specials |
| 10:45 | Social Studies |
| 11:15 | Lunch |
| 11:45 | Math |
| 12:15 | Science |
| 12:45 | Science/Health/Media |
| 1:30 | Recess |
| 2:00 | Dismissal |

In this 6-hour day, 2 hours and 30 minutes is dedicated to reading, writing, and math. That's 41% of the day, or less than half of the school day that is dedicated to core skills. One could argue that if the content of science, social studies, health, media, and specials works to incorporate reading and writing (and maybe math) in daily practice, then really the percentage is much higher. In reality, it's a tough push to ensure that all teachers are adequately addressing their literacy standards, and usually these non-ELA subjects are reading-free zones.

Take a look at Sample Elementary Schedule B:

Table 8.2 Sample Elementary Schedule B

| 8:00 | Arrival, Morning Meetings |
|-------|----------------------------|
| 8:15 | LA/Writing Block |
| 9:00 | Math Block |
| 10:00 | Specials |
| 11:00 | Reading Block |
| 12:30 | Lunch and Recess |
| 1:30 | Science/Social Studies/Intervention |
| 2:00 | Dismissal |

In the second sample schedule, 54% of the daily schedule is devoted to reading, writing, and math. Intervention ELA and math is built into the science/social studies block, and students are still experiencing an hour of specials (art, music, PE/health, computer, library) each day. There is over an hour for lunch, recess, and morning meetings, all of which support the social-emotional needs of students (more to come on this topic later in the chapter).

It doesn't take much to create a schedule that prioritizes your learning goals. You just have to do it. Often taking that action is the difficult step, as building and district leaders, quite honestly, fear repercussions from their staff. Just because a school has always had a certain schedule does not mean leaders should continue to misallocate the precious classroom time of their students. Changing the schedule is a simple, doable, necessary support that benefits all students. But then, make this the norm across your district.

The next step is to search for space within the schedule where interventions can occur. Our examples place intervention time during the science/social studies block. The best interventions are timely, responsive, and specific to student needs. Reading and math are the critical watch areas, and schools need to create specific curricula that addresses student deficits.

It's also not enough to just have the time, space, and curriculum—the best interventions are taught by certified teachers or highly qualified instructional aides who have been trained in best practice intervention techniques. We are not going to dive into specifics with what to do in terms of intervention (because schools vary in their instructional approaches), but we can tell you that computer-based intervention is not going to help your students make the gains that they desire. You cannot replace a physical teacher with a screen and expect to create the same levels of engagement and learning. When looking to adopt new resources for your curriculum, ask questions about intervention and tiered materials. And, make sure these materials are standards-based (just like your core curriculum). Then, ensure your staff understands *how* to use these materials with the students.

Small groups, frequent checks for understanding, choral responses, and other high-engagement techniques are instructional strategies that anyone can utilize—if asked to. Our advice is to avoid the flashy new toys, the bells and whistles, the gimmicky "of the moment" ideas on how to best reach struggling learners. Remember: basic doesn't have to mean boring.

Determining which students need an intervention can be a difficult task. We recommend using the math concept of a J Curve as you explain intervention steps to your staff.

In Brownsburg, new teachers see this visual each year on their very first induction day. We revisit the principles each year during our PLC leadership summit. It is, once again, a running thread that anchors our approach to intervention.

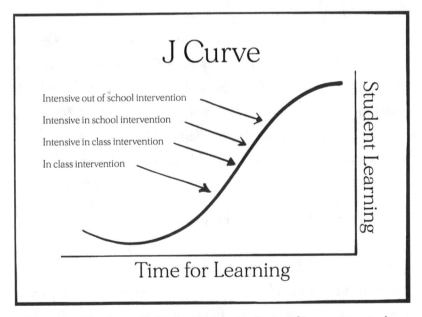

**Figure 8.1:** The Approach Used to Determine Stages of Intervention in the RTI Process

The best way to support all of your students academically is to ensure the strength and competency of your instructional staff. The next support is to equip the staff with a common, viable curriculum that has built-in, purposeful assessments. The assessments can allow staff to determine interventions (when needed) for specific students. As students progress through the RTI process, more time in (and eventually out of) school may be required. An additional intervention period solves the issues of a built-in intensive in-school intervention. Intensive out-of-school interventions may take the appearance of after-school reading clubs or before-school practice with teachers. Independent computer work (even if done at school) does not qualify as intensive intervention.

But again, the key factor to consider with the J Curve is what can be done to differentiate learning within the regularly scheduled class time for students?

School and district leaders need to equip teachers with practical, actionable, differentiation strategies that can be used daily. If differentiation feels cumbersome and daunting, teachers are likely going to avoid it at all costs. Likewise, if differentiation equates to more work for similar results, teachers will burn themselves out in an attempt to meet expectations. It's up to the district and building leaders to properly support teachers' desires to differentiate.

When possible, co-teaching structures in classes are the best way to assist both students who need extra support. Two teachers can absolutely differentiate material and learning environments easier than one (though we argue one teacher can be highly effective at it as well). When working with students with IEPs, often the greatest accommodation we can provide is the awareness of the teachers to create small, specialized (or differentiated) settings.

Another important support investment is to add instructional coaches to your elementary buildings. Some schools provide a coach for each grade level across a district; others assign a coach to a particular building. In addition to traditional coaching roles, some districts have created specialized coaches for specific departments, such as special education, life skills, and related arts.

The coach serves as the instructional support to teachers. As such, the coach can provide ideas and structures for differentiation when needed. They can push into the classroom to help with stations, small groups, and specially designed instruction. The coach can work with co-teachers to find the much-needed balance of two teaching adults in the room. The coach can also assist in the planning and implementation of highly impactful lessons. Having a coach is one thing, but training a coach to be impactful is another. Step one is allocating resources to create coaches. Step two is to train, support, and empower these coaches.

## Secondary Academic Supports

Middle school is a critically important transition period for most students. Often, academic struggles from elementary years follow right into the middle, and that means that leaders need to prepare varying support systems for grades 6–8, too.

In Brownsburg, the number one way we support our middle school students is to assign them to structured teams of teachers who serve as students' home base throughout each year. Each team consists of an English, math, science, and social studies teacher, and where needed, special education and ENL staff join as well. Many middle schools choose to create team atmospheres for their middle school students, and though it is not always the most convenient option in terms of staffing and scheduling, we do believe it to be the most supportive option for students.

To help ease the transition, our sixth-grade teams are smaller, consisting of two or three core teachers instead of four. At the sixth-grade level, classes are 87 minutes in length and one or two teachers teach more than one subject area. The increased length of course class time allows for more in-class interventions and small-group time to occur, and it also eases the social tension by transitioning between fewer classrooms throughout the day.

By the seventh- and eighth-grade years, students are assigned to teams of four content-area teachers, and classes are 63 minutes in length. The seventh- and eighth-grade teams do not function in a block schedule, yet Tier I interventions and small-group supports are still expected to occur on a regular basis at these levels. The Tight-Loose-Tight philosophy really supports in-class interventions for our secondary students because teachers are able to appropriately plan re-teach or small-group time in their well-established units. Secondary teachers must become masters at adjusting classroom activities such as bell-ringers or stations to fit the needs of all learners. These teachers (like the elementary as well) look for pockets of classroom time to pull students who need more feedback or practice before moving them on with the rest of the class.

Co-teaching models are vital at the secondary level as well, and special education and ENL teachers loop with their students year-to-year. At the end of the day, the connection between teacher of record (TOR) and student trumps the connection among teacher staff or content experience.

In addition to the teaming concept at our middle levels, there is also a built-in Tier II intervention time to support students' learning needs. The middle schools refer to this time as SEEK, Student Enrichment and Extension of Knowledge. The purpose of this 45-minute class is to provide students the necessary time to get intervention or enrichment in their academic areas of need. All English, math, and special education teachers teach intervention SEEKs while social studies, science, and fine arts teachers have enrichment groups. The intervention classes are small, averaging between 10 and 15 students in a group, while the enrichment SEEKs are large (sometimes nearly 35 in a class). In eighth grade, students are able to test into Level I foreign language courses instead of taking science or social studies SEEK.

SEEK placement is determined by data dives conducted by teachers and administrators each summer. State assessment scores drive much of the placement for intervention SEEK lists, and students' social and emotional needs are also considered while scheduling students.

In short, the purpose of SEEK is to provide students with specific, individualized intervention for reading, writing, and math. Brownsburg does not use a unified program to provide interventions to all students; rather, teachers respond to the needs of students, often creating or finding curriculum from multiple sources. The beauty of a class like SEEK is that it is designed to meet the varying needs of students. The difficulty is that no two students are exactly alike, so often teachers feel as if they're in a guessing game in terms of instructional strategies that work.

Data is tracked to progress monitor the growth of students, and teachers are again given guidance on how to meaningful use this data. Because SEEK is responsive to students' needs by nature, the two middle schools do not necessarily track data the same way, nor should they. Likewise, though the elementary schools all have a reading and math lab structure, not all schools have the same instructional practices during lab. Providing the time for these interventions is tight; the instructional practices of interventions are loose.

Additionally, assistant principals and guidance counselors pair together to loop with grade levels to provide ongoing academic support to students and families. Teams hold weekly meetings to discuss academic and social-emotional concerns about students, and counselors and assistant principals rotate through these meetings on a bimonthly basis to maintain communication and follow-through.

The power of teaming can only occur if there is constant, clear communication among all parties. Relationships are the key to success in any organization, but this is especially true in schools. The teaming structures create the sense of true belonging for our students. Our students desire to know they are worth the extra time and energy—the extra meeting, the conference, the new game plan. If you structure your secondary supports so that teams exist but do not ensure there is clear, consistent communication among all stakeholders, the impact of the system will be minimal.

Relationships are perhaps most important during high school years (and often the most difficult to maintain). At the high school level, students experience 50-minute class periods in a traditional seven-period day. Unlike most high schools, students keep the same teacher for year-long courses rather than swapping at semester. Again, intentional decisions—like teacher consistency and bell schedules—are simple, manageable systemic decisions that make a lasting impact on relationships and learning.

Like both the elementary and middle school systems, Tier I interventions are expected to occur during the 50-minute class period, and teachers continually seek out ways to meaningfully differentiate higher-level content. The PLC support network is crucial, and teachers work together to address concerns and needs of students. The key to academic support is to respond as quickly and intentionally as possible—with researched-based strategies. The high school PLCs meet every other week, and high school teachers rarely teach more than two preps (while many teach only one). The two prep maximum allows for quality impact on learning in each PLC.

Teaming also has a place at the high school, albeit in a somewhat different format. Assistant principals essentially serve as principals of their designated grade level, and they lead their students for four years—from freshman year to graduation. Each grade-level team consists of an assistant principal, two guidance counselors, an academic coach, an administrative assistant, two special education teachers. In 2019, as we wrote this book, Brownsburg High School had roughly 2,800 students enrolled for the 2019–2020 year. Each grade averages between 650 and 750 students, which means there are eight adults assigned specifically to get to know their students for the next four years. The goal of each team is clear: build relationships and support each individual student on their path to graduation and beyond.

If you are responsible for leading within a large high school, consider the various ways you can make your school feel smaller and more relational for your students. We readily admit that this system works for Brownsburg because of its current size; to afford four assistant principals in a school with 400 students is not only unlikely but also unnecessary. The key to teams is that you have a set group of people who are responsible for one another. Consider this: when parents have a question, they know exactly who to contact and who they will speak with. If a teacher needs support with a student, he knows which assistant principal or counselor to contact and why. And most importantly, when students themselves feel overwhelmed, frustrated, lost, excited, happy, and celebratory, they know which group of people to share their feelings with.

Teams can exist beyond our athletic fields and sporting arenas, and we urge you to consider the various ways you can create these support networks in your schools. Perhaps you already have some of these pieces or could leverage staffing or funding to slowly create this team. There are ways to work with what you have or reimagine staffing structure to creatively connect with kids. The safety net can exist; you just might have to make the rope first.

Effective teams provide the individualized RTI support that their students need, and without purposeful connection, far too many of our youth today are fighting a losing battle to apathy, disconnect, and despair.

## Elementary Social-Emotional Supports

With seven elementary schools, consistency in support is key to providing equity for our students. Each elementary school has one counselor, and this counselor works with students K–5. Counselors create lessons and small groups to instruct students about the seven character traits that Brownsburg focuses on K–12: respect, responsibility, compassion, integrity, perseverance, acceptance, and citizenship.

With a purposeful focus on systems and alignment, it can be hard to identify moments when a system is missing or needed. What, then, do you do if a need is identified? What's the process?

In 2017, we faced this exact dilemma specifically in our K–1 classrooms. Through quarterly grade-level check-in meetings between PLC leaders and the central office team, a rising concern about emotional preparedness for school was identified. Teachers shared that more and more of their students seemed emotionally ill-equipped to handle expectations and relationships at school, and there was a growing need to support social skills, too.

Schools and principals were singularly addressing concerns with students, and on their own they attempted to address the growing needs. Without a clear system or process to follow, inequity in support could develop and so the leaders determined a different plan.

Rather than immediately adopting a program (or several) to fix the concern, a team of K–1 teachers and counselors worked together to review potential resources that could strengthen staff members' abilities to connect with students. The resource that was adopted is honestly irrelevant in the situation. What is essential is that the leaders developed a process for a team to choose one common tool. Providing one common go-to resource would ensure equity for students from all teachers, in all buildings, and would also make the evaluation of the tool more effective.

The resource was selected in 2018 and the following school year teachers were provided optional training in the summer, but then also follow-up support throughout the year. The goal of the training was not to implement a grand, sweeping new program, but rather to encourage teachers to see that simply making a tweak here or there to conversations, greetings, and interactions could go a long way in developing the safe learning environments they sought to create.

To be fair, Brownsburg does not do anything unique or unusual in regard to the social-emotional support it provides elementary students. Teachers focus heavily on relationship building, and they continue to refine their abilities to connect with their students. Now, they simply do so more systematically.

## Secondary Social-Emotional Supports

Today's society offers a wide variety of experiences to our tweens and teens. Social media, online streaming, and smartphones all provide ample opportunities for our kids to connect (and disconnect) more than nearly all adults serving in the field of education. It's imperative that schools put a high-priority focus on the social-emotional needs of their students. Relationships are key in supporting anyone's emotional well-being, and it's time we as school leaders push ourselves to prioritize this health need above scores and reports.

People, not programs is a common mantra we explored previously in Chapter 3. Though we admit Brownsburg Schools could and should do even more to provide specialized support for its students, we also believe we are on the right path in focusing on relationships between students and staff. To support the growing needs of our middle and high school students, the primary focus once again turns to teaming structures at both levels.

Both middle schools utilize the teaming approach in grades 6–8 to ensure that all students have a "home base" of teachers who will know, share, and support them throughout the year. At the sixth-grade level, teams consist of two or three teachers to provide fewer transitions (and less stress) during this year. Teams at the seventh and eighth grades consist of four core teachers. Each team has a designated teacher-leader who is the primary connection between the team and parents. When concerns arise (either academic or behavioral in nature), it is often the team leader who arranges for parent meetings or discussions. The team leader also guides team meetings with students.

One counselor is assigned to each grade level, and counselors loop with their students for all three years of middle school. This close connection allows for students, teachers, and administrators to trust that the counselors truly know their students and can offer the best support possible.

Consider your system once more:

⟶ Are there simple, high-impact changes you can make to your organization of staff to better connect students with the adults in their school?
⟶ What can you rearrange to show where your priorities are in student wellness?

In addition to the relationship structure, both middle schools also carry on the focus on character education. One piece of this instruction is that students participate in weekly character lessons during their SEEK (intervention/enrichment period).

Like many schools around the country, East and West middle schools also implement effective Positive Behavior Intervention Support , or PBIS, systems and utilize restorative justice practices with students.

When needed, small groups are created by counselors and gender-specific groups work with at-risk students on leadership, citizenship, and confidence.

At the high school, the teaming concept again takes the lead in providing social-emotional support for students. Each grade (or team) has two counselors who loop with their students for all four years. On a larger scale, students in Brownsburg hypothetically have three counselors throughout their 13 years of education: one at elementary, one in middle school, and one in high school. The looping system with counselors allows for students to have a stronger sense of belonging and connection with their school and community.

Teachers and aides provide the first line of social-emotional supports for our students. When all staff members firmly believe in student-centered learning, they choose to act on behalf of their students' best interests. In Brownsburg, it is expected that teachers build strong relationships with all of their students. Are there some students who are hard to love? Absolutely. Still, all staff know, deep down, that this is a district full of people who love the kids. When you create a culture where staff know they are expected to love the kids, a funny thing happens: the adults truly do love the kids. And because of this, incredibly strong relationships exist between teachers and students.

When teachers and staff are connected to their students, social-emotional cues and warning signs are more easily spotted and addressed. All the programs in the world will never replace the power of connection between a child and her teacher. When students know that their teachers genuinely care about them, they feel safe and, in this vulnerability, there is opportunity for growth, learning, and wellness.

Chapter 9:

# The Proof Is in the Pudding

"What gets measured (and clearly
defined) does get done."

– Mike Schmoker

How do you know if the systems or methods we suggest throughout this book will meet the needs of your students, your teachers, your leaders, your parents, your community, your situation?

What actually works is a question that all educators around the world are attempting to answer. In the name of this pursuit, districts add initiative after initiative; training after training; program after program.

When you think you're adding a new idea (and it's replacing an old one), we caution you to think twice. Usually teachers view the new idea as an add-on, not a replacement behavior. It's *difficult* to change behaviors that are well-established in routines, classrooms, and buildings. If you want to create sustainable clarity, clear the table and start fresh.

John Hattie's Visible Learning research should become an absolute cornerstone in our decision-making about what influences student achievement. Hattie's ongoing, decades-long research reveals the answer to the question. In 2017, collective teacher efficacy was the second most impactful influence on student achievement. In 2019, it was the first. And what is collective teacher efficacy? In short, an effective PLC process.

When teachers are given the time, expectation, support, and accountability to make the best decisions based on data, they are able to make the greatest impact on student learning.

One unique aspect of the Brownsburg story is that the common focus was applied not only across an entire school but an entire district. Leaders relentlessly carry the Burden of No when new suggestions and initiatives arise. What you typically see in educational leadership books are singleton schools that have applied these focused principles; you rarely see this play out in an entire district.

## Longitudinal State Assessment Data

Educators around the world are in agreement that standardized tests are one measurement tool among many in the analysis toolkit of school and district quality. Data and numbers are easily manipulated, and they can easily hide what you don't see in a district as much as what you do see.

We know, for example, that higher poverty rates in a school or district tend to translate into lower achievement rates on standardized tests. Attendance, transience, homelessness, and family situations also impact the emotional security of our students, which of course impacts their experiences in the classroom.

Poverty, not race nor language nor gender, is the greatest societal influence on whether or not a student achieves grade-level or above benchmarks on standardized measures. Research has unfortunately shown that "students from low income families consistently, regardless of ethnicity or race, score well below average" (Bergeson, 2006).

This is not to suggest, however, that all schools or districts with higher poverty levels are automatically faced with a glass ceiling on achievement. Quite the contrary. In fact, one of the greatest arguments we hope to present in this book is to convince our educational leaders that clarity, accountability, and collective teacher efficacy are the true tools needed to equip teachers to make the greatest gains possible for our students from disadvantaged backgrounds.

In Indiana, third through eighth graders, along with 10th graders, take a yearly state assessment that measures achievement in math, languages, and in varying years science and social studies. Table 9.1 shows the progression of achievement on the ISTEP test *across the district.*

Table 9.1 Longitudinal State Assessment Data

| Brownsburg Community School Corporation-Trend Data | | | | | | | |
|---|---|---|---|---|---|---|---|
| ELA | | Math | | Both ELA & Math | | Official State Rank | |
| Year | District Passing % | Year | District Passing % | Year | District Passing % | Year | Rank |
| 1996 | 77.1 | 1996 | 77.1 | 1996 | | 1996 | |
| 1997 | 81.5 | 1997 | 78.2 | 1997 | | 1997 | |
| 1998 | 83.2 | 1998 | 80.1 | 1998 | | 1998 | |
| 1999 | 79.5 | 1999 | 81.1 | 1999 | | 1999 | |
| 2000 | 80.8 | 2000 | 84.7 | 2000 | | 2000 | |
| 2001 | 80.0 | 2001 | 83.5 | 2001 | | 2001 | |
| 2002 | 81.8 | 2002 | 82.7 | 2002 | | 2002 | |
| 2003 | 83.4 | 2003 | 84.3 | 2003 | | 2003 | |
| 2004 | 83.8 | 2004 | 85.2 | 2004 | | 2004 | |
| 2005 | 82.7 | 2005 | 86.0 | 2005 | 78.0 | 2005 | 21 |
| 2006 | 83.1 | 2006 | 85.7 | 2006 | 78.4 | 2006 | 22 |
| 2007 | 83.1 | 2007 | 84.7 | 2007 | 77.6 | 2007 | 23 |
| 2008F | 81.5 | 2008F | 83.6 | 2008F | 75.8 | 2008F | 31 |
| 2009S | 82.3 | 2009S | 82.3 | 2009S | 76.4 | 2009S | 21 |
| 2010S | 85.3 | 2010S | 88.1 | 2010S | 81.1 | 2010S | 18 |
| 2011 | 86.9 | 2011 | 90.4 | 2011 | 84.9 | 2011 | 17 |
| 2012 | 90.0 | 2012 | 93.2 | 2012 | 88.3 | 2012 | 5 |
| 2013 | 91.4 | 2013 | 94.8 | 2013 | 89.4 | 2013 | 5 |
| 2014 | 91.8 | 2014 | 95.9 | 2014 | 90.5 | 2014 | 6 |
| 2015* | 85.6% | 2015 | 86.4% | 2015 | 79.7% | 2015 | 3 |
| 2016** | 87.2% | 2016 | 88.0% | 2016 | 82.1% | 2016 | 1 |
| 2017** | 88.3% | 2017 | 88.0% | 2017 | 83.1% | 2017 | 1 |
| 2018** | 88.5% | 2018 | 89.2% | 2018 | 83.6% | 2018 | 1 |
| *2015 ISTEP+ recut to CCR standards | | | | | | | |
| **2016 ISTEP+ does not include grade 10 | | | | | | | |

This data ends in 2018 because the state transitioned to a new measurement tool, ILEARN. The coloring between 1996 and 2014 shows a steady progression of achievement on the ISTEP test. The district began its streamlined PLC process in 2011, and in 2012 huge performance gains occurred. The pass rates for math were slightly higher than language arts, an occurrence almost entirely unheard of in most districts.

In 2015, the ISTEP test became more rigorous, reflecting the newly adopted Indiana State Standards (which closely align with the Common Core). Though the percentage passing dipped in the initial year, performance in terms of rank improved. In other words, students in Brownsburg outperformed more students across the state as the test became more complex.

Between 2016 and 2018, Brownsburg students, as a district, were the top-performing students in math, language arts, and students passing both—in the entire state of Indiana.

Then, in 2019 (the only existing data for ILEARN) Brownsburg was once again the highest-performing district in both math, language arts, and students passing both tests. Brownsburg also experienced the smallest drop on the test (when comparing passing percentage of ISTEP to ILEARN).

For the past four years, when only looking at state standardized tests, Brownsburg has been the highest-performing district in the state.

And what about results on national tests or AP tests? When we look at Table 9.2, we see there has been a steady trend of students passing (earning a 3, 4, or 5) on AP tests in the district.

Table 9.2 AP Test Results

| | Total of AP Students | Number of Exams | Students with 3+ Scores | % of Students with Scores 3+ |
|---|---|---|---|---|
| 2016 | 498 | 823 | 369 | 74.1 |
| 2017 | 583 | 975 | 441 | 75.6 |
| 2018 | 634 | 1140 | 495 | 78.1 |
| 2019 | 741 | 1329 | 548 | 74.0 |
| 2020 | 662 | 1187 | 508 | 76.7 |

When we compare the growth from 2016 to 2020, and again this is only half of the time that Brownsburg has utilized the PLC process district-wide, we see 164 more students taking AP tests, 364 more tests taken, 139 more students passing these exams, and an increase in the percentage of students passing, too.

Translation: more students are taking *and passing* more tests.

Or, to borrow the common educational phrase, "A rising tide lifts all boats."

## More Layers

But, of course, there is more. Though not an economically disadvantaged district, nearly 23% of students in Brownsburg schools receive free and reduced-price lunches. This is nearly double, and in some cases quadruple the poverty rates of the second- and third-ranked districts in the state. If poverty rate alone determined achievement, then Brownsburg should be somewhere in the teens or twenties in terms of achievement on tests.

And we used to be—before the implementation of *Tight-Loose-Tight*; similar-to-identical practices; an emphasis on people, not programs; and critical teacher-coaching supports and PLCs that ensure our teachers are the most expert in the field.

We started this chapter by acknowledging the obvious truth that standardized tests are only one measurement tool, and rarely, if ever, do they show the entire story.

Next, let's take a look at graduation rates.

Before the teaming model was implemented at the high school, graduation rates, though still above the state average, were 92.1%. But after teams? Graduation rates rose. In 2014, four years after the implementation of teaming and the PLC process, the graduation rate jumped to 98.6% (see Table 9.2).

Table 9.3 Graduation Rates' Growth from 2010 to 2020

Students were supported by specific leaders who were hired to coach, mentor, and guide them. People, not programs, helped students to stay in school and earn their diplomas. People, not programs, worked with students after school to make-up or re-do assignments for credit eligibility. People, not programs, take great pride in our graduates every year as they walk across the stage.

## But, Is This System Truly Equitable?

We often tell our teachers to look critically at what the data is and is not saying. For example, the ISTEP data alone does not reveal how certain demographics or subgroups perform in relation to peers. The data does not show how many students, year after year, continue to experience failure. The data does not show how many students have experienced emotional trauma, abuse, bullying, racism, sexual harassment, homelessness, disordered thinking, anxiety, depression, and suicidal thoughts.

The data also does not show the culture of each building or the value felt of each teacher.

Five years into the sustainable PLC process, the leadership team began asking questions about equity, gaps, and missed information. Rather than setting achievement goals for school improvement plans, we set gap-narrowing goals. We analyzed how many students were held "at core" or grade level from year to year, and we searched for trends (whether positive or negative) within the data.

Through the critical lens, we discovered that our non-white students were disproportionately under-enrolled in high-ability, dual-credit, and AP courses. We realized that in most of our schools, our students with IEPs were drastically underperforming compared to their peers who did not receive support services. We also realized that a few of our elementary schools essentially eliminated an achievement gap in this area, and we then had to dig in and figure out exactly how they did it. With so many pieces of our system similar to identical, outlier data must be explored to learn the nuances that ultimately make the difference.

In some schools, students impacted by poverty more greatly underperformed, while in other schools the gap did not exist at all.

We continued to examine hidden gaps and possible gaps. We led community members to make conscious decisions when they

redistricted to ensure poverty rates did not become dispropor-
tionate in one school over another.

What's key to note is that never, even once the district became
the highest performing in the state, did the teachers or leaders
believe the work to improve was done. Never was the goal to earn
a number one position. The goal has always been educating our
students—all of our students—to the best of our abilities.

## Blind Spots

The work on narrowing the gaps continues, and depending on
the year, the gaps with groups will shift. With a continued focus
on systems and clarity, teachers are empowered to make real-time
decisions that support their students.

Sometimes, however, we have found that the constant focus,
the extreme clarity, the Burden of No can inadvertently create
what we lovingly refer to as *blind spots*.

There's an exercise that was originally conducted by Daniel
Simons and Christopher Chabris. In the exercise, they record a
group of people passing a basketball within a circle. As a viewer, you
are instructed to count how many times the people pass the ball.

While you are counting, a person in a gorilla suit walks
through the room.

Here's what the scientists discovered: very few people notice
the gorilla. It isn't until the end, when they are told that a gorilla
walked through, that viewers even know it happened. In disbe-
lief, most people re-watch the video and sure enough, the second

time through—*when they know they should look for the gorilla*—they spot it.

We have found that if you aren't careful, you can become so entrenched, so insulated, so narrowed that you completely miss the gorilla as it walks through your room.

Blind spots can prevent leaders from:

➠ digging more critically into data that seems positive or encouraging on the surface;

➠ learning from other districts about their strengths, skills, and success;

➠ addressing concerns with your leaders, especially if you've worked with your team for a considerable amount of time;

➠ showing vulnerability, owning mistakes, or empowering other leaders;

➠ addressing cultural or societal issues;

➠ altering a system (or stopping it altogether) if it proves ineffective over time; and

➠ supporting certain pockets of teachers or departments who do need more specialized professional development, coaching, or guidance.

Blind spots, in short, can deteriorate the culture you work so hard and long to build.

Creating a sustainable, aligned system within your district is paramount to ensure teacher, leader, and student success. But if you do not also build in reflection and feedback, systems of transparency and accountability, your blind spots will cause you to miss your mark every time.

So what do we do?

How do we, as leaders, create the kind of atmosphere needed where our staff is comfortable and encouraged to notice the blind spots?

How do you seek out who Edward de Bono refers to as Black Hat thinkers—those team members who are willing to play devil's advocate, to question the decision, to look at the situation from unexplored angles and new perspectives?

How do you embrace diverse perspectives, critical perspectives, and truly shared leadership?

How do you build a system that can spot the blind spots?

## A Final Thought

Teachers are begging for school leaders who are courageous enough to simplify the system. Ask any of your teachers and they'll tell you: in order to sustain, they must believe they are making an impact.

When too many plates are spinning—when too many initiatives are present—teachers sink in the confusion and lack of clarity from leadership. Programs muddy the water of what works and what doesn't, and when teachers cannot see their impact, they leave the profession.

If you are a leader of any kind in your school or district, you have the power and influence to help simplify the system. It all starts with courageous conversations about what is needed and what matters.

The Burden of No is a heavy burden to bear, but one we urge you to adopt as part of your leadership philosophy. You owe it to your teachers to protect their time and energy. By saying no to new initiatives and programs, you create prioritized time for instructional refinement of curriculum and assessment.

Professional learning communities create collective efficacy. John Hattie's research reveals **collective teacher efficacy** to be the most influential instructional framework that exists in education. Period. Ignoring the research behind the impact of teacher collective efficacy is borderline educational neglect.

We wrote this book to share the story of what is possible if leaders decide to avoid the frills and flares and instead focus back in on people, not programs. Research tells us, time and time again, that relationships and trust are what lead to learning and growth. This is true for students and teachers alike.

If you want to take bold, audacious steps to improving school leadership, be simple. Eliminate most, if not all, of the programs and initiatives weighing down your teachers. Make clear the learning priorities for your students, and create a system that protects this. Fight the urge to jump on the new bandwagon or adopt the next piece of tech. Your teachers are begging you to simplify, simplify, simplify.

Have the courage to say less is more. Eliminate unnecessary arrows, and align the ones that remain. Empower your teachers to embrace this mantra and then provide them with talented staff who can coach them on lesson design, curriculum creation, and data analysis.

Teachers want to impact student learning. They want to do their best. It's your job to create a system that will let them.

# Glossary

**Collective teacher efficacy**—Collective teacher efficacy refers to a shared belief held among a group of educators that their collective effort will impact the outcome of a task, event, or goal.

**Culture of dignity**—A school culture that creates and values dignity for all students and staff. A culture of dignity creates affirmation, validation, acceptance, and equity.

**Data and testing coordinator**—This is an administrative position located at our central office. The responsibilities of this position include the coordination of state testing for our district, creator of student data rosters, and completing data mining requests for administrators and teachers in the district.

**Formative assessment**—Formative assessment refers to a wide variety of methods that teachers use to conduct in-process check-ins of student comprehension, learning needs, and academic progress during a lesson, unit, or course. In other words, formative assessments are for learning.

**J Curve**—J Curve is an educational idea that as time increases, the likelihood of student learning increases as well. (See Figure 8.1, in Chapter 8)

**Leverage point**—In systems thinking, a leverage point is a place in a system's structure where a solution element can be applied. It's a low leverage point if a small amount of change force causes a small change in system behavior. It's a high leverage point if a small amount of change force causes a large change in system behavior.

**People, Not Programs**—A philosophical approach to district leadership and initiatives. This idea places development emphasis on people, not adoptions, programs, or new ideas.

**PLC Leadership Summit**—A day of professional development and realignment of our vision for PLCs. Attendees include PLC leaders and building administration.

**Professional Learning Communities (PLCs)**—Professional learning communities are teams. They create a method to foster collaborative learning among colleagues within a particular work environment or field. It is often used in schools as a way to organize teachers into working groups of practice-based professional learning for student growth.

**Purposeful redundancy**—Common expectations that are clearly articulated and taught to all stakeholders.

**RTI**—Response to Intervention (RTI) is a multi-tier approach to the early identification and support of students with learning and behavior needs. All students receive high-quality, research-based instruction in the general education classroom. Ongoing student assessment is used to progress monitor.

**Secondary department head (SDH)**—A curriculum administrator role, overseeing teachers in their content area in grades 6–12. Hiring, coaching, evaluating, curriculum and assessment work, professional development, and overseeing PLCs in their content area are the main responsibilities.

**Similar to identical**—Belief that two or more aspects (curriculum, assessments, teacher evaluations, process across buildings, etc.) are monitored inside of a system that promotes commonalities over individualism.

**Summative assessment**—The goal of summative assessment is to evaluate student learning at the end of an instructional unit by comparing it against some standard or benchmark. Summative assessments are often high stakes (e.g., Unit Test, Project, Final Exam).

**The Burden of No**—When faced with the task of aligning structures within systems, district leaders must shoulder the Burden of No as they are frequently asked to invest in new ideas, initiatives, and programs. Leaders must be ready to say no, and this can feel cumbersome and difficult.

*Tight-Loose-Tight*—Common Curriculum (Tight), Art of Teaching/Facilitating Learning (Loose), and Common Summative Assessments (Tight).

# Appendix

# A1: Longitudinal State Assessment Data

| Brownsburg Community School Corporation-Trend Data | | | | | | | |
|---|---|---|---|---|---|---|---|
| ELA | | Math | | Both ELA & Math | | Official State Rank | |
| Year | District Passing % | Year | District Passing % | Year | District Passing % | Year | Rank |
| 1996 | 77.1 | 1996 | 77.1 | 1996 | | 1996 | |
| 1997 | 81.5 | 1997 | 78.2 | 1997 | | 1997 | |
| 1998 | 83.2 | 1998 | 80.1 | 1998 | | 1998 | |
| 1999 | 79.5 | 1999 | 81.1 | 1999 | | 1999 | |
| 2000 | 80.8 | 2000 | 84.7 | 2000 | | 2000 | |
| 2001 | 80.0 | 2001 | 83.5 | 2001 | | 2001 | |
| 2002 | 81.8 | 2002 | 82.7 | 2002 | | 2002 | |
| 2003 | 83.4 | 2003 | 84.3 | 2003 | | 2003 | |
| 2004 | 83.8 | 2004 | 85.2 | 2004 | | 2004 | |
| 2005 | 82.7 | 2005 | 86.0 | 2005 | 78.0 | 2005 | 21 |
| 2006 | 83.1 | 2006 | 85.7 | 2006 | 78.4 | 2006 | 22 |
| 2007 | 83.1 | 2007 | 84.7 | 2007 | 77.6 | 2007 | 23 |
| 2008F | 81.5 | 2008F | 83.6 | 2008F | 75.8 | 2008F | 31 |
| 2009S | 82.3 | 2009S | 82.3 | 2009S | 76.4 | 2009S | 21 |
| 2010S | 85.3 | 2010S | 88.1 | 2010S | 81.1 | 2010S | 18 |
| 2011 | 86.9 | 2011 | 90.4 | 2011 | 84.9 | 2011 | 17 |
| 2012 | 90.0 | 2012 | 93.2 | 2012 | 88.3 | 2012 | 5 |
| 2013 | 91.4 | 2013 | 94.8 | 2013 | 89.4 | 2013 | 5 |
| 2014 | 91.8 | 2014 | 95.9 | 2014 | 90.5 | 2014 | 6 |
| 2015* | 85.6% | 2015 | 86.4% | 2015 | 79.7% | 2015 | 3 |
| 2016** | 87.2% | 2016 | 88.0% | 2016 | 82.1% | 2016 | 1 |
| 2017** | 88.3% | 2017 | 88.0% | 2017 | 83.1% | 2017 | 1 |
| 2018** | 88.5% | 2018 | 89.2% | 2018 | 83.6% | 2018 | 1 |
| *2015 ISTEP+ recut to CCR standards | | | | | | | |
| **2016 ISTEP+ does not include grade 10 | | | | | | | |

# B1: PLC Evaluation Process

## DOMAIN 4: PLANNING AND PREPARATION FOR LEARNING

| Indicator 4a | The teacher utilizes assessment data to plan and drive instruction. |
|---|---|
| Highly Effective (Level 4) | A teacher fulfills the criteria for Effective and: <br><br> Incorporates differentiated instructional strategies in planning to reach every student at his/her level of understanding; and <br><br> Persists in the search of effective approaches for students who lack success. |
| Effective (Level 3) | Teacher uses prior assessment data to formulate: <br><br> Design of achievement goals, unit plans, and lesson plans. |
| Improvement Necessary (Level 2) | Teacher uses prior assessment data to formulate: <br><br> Design of achievement goals, unit plans, or lesson plans, but not all of the above. |
| Ineffective (Level 1) | Teacher rarely or never uses prior assessment data when planning. |

| Indicator 4b | The teacher collaborates with grade-level/subject-area colleagues during PLC to develop best educational practices. |
|---|---|
| Highly Effective (Level 4) | A teacher fulfills the criteria for Effective and additionally may: <br><br> Go above and beyond in seeking out opportunities to collaborate; <br><br> Coach peers through difficult situations; and <br><br> Take on leadership roles within collaborative groups such as PLCs. |
| Effective (Level 3) | Teacher will: <br><br> Seek out and participate in regular opportunities to work with and learn from others; and <br><br> Ask for assistance, when needed, and provide assistance to others in need. |
| Improvement Necessary (Level 2) | Teacher will: <br><br> Participate in occasional opportunities to work with and learn from others; and <br><br> Ask for assistance when needed. <br><br> Teacher may not: <br><br> Seek to provide other teachers with assistance when needed; and/or Regularly seek out opportunities to work with others. |
| Ineffective (Level 1) | Teacher rarely or never participates in opportunities to work with others. <br><br> Teacher works in isolation and is not a team player. |

| Indicator 4c | The teacher creates objective-driven lesson plans and assessments. |
|---|---|
| **Highly Effective (Level 4)** | A teacher fulfills the criteria for Effective and additionally: <br><br> Plans for a variety of differentiated instructional strategies, anticipating where these will be needed to enhance instruction; and <br><br> Incorporates a variety of informal assessments/checks for understanding as well as summative assessments where necessary and uses all assessments to directly inform instruction. |
| **Effective (Level 3)** | Based on unit plan, teacher plans daily lessons by: <br><br> Identifying lesson objectives that are aligned to state content standards; <br><br> Matching instructional strategies as well as meaningful and relevant activities/assignments to the lesson objectives; and <br><br> Designing formative assessments that measure progress toward mastery and inform instruction. |
| **Improvement Necessary (Level 2)** | Based on unit plan, teacher plans daily lessons by: <br><br> Identifying lesson objectives that are aligned to state content standards; and <br><br> Matching instructional strategies and activities/assignments to the lesson objectives. <br><br> Teacher may not: <br><br> Design assignments that are meaningful or relevant; and/or <br><br> Plan formative assessments to measure progress toward mastery or inform instruction. |
| **Ineffective (Level 1)** | Teacher rarely or never plans daily lessons or daily lessons are planned but are thrown together at the last minute, thus lacking meaningful objectives, instructional strategies, or assignments. |
| Indicator 4d | The teacher develops standards-based unit plans and assessments. |
| **Highly Effective (Level 4)** | A teacher fulfills the criteria for Effective and additionally: <br><br> Creates well-designed unit assessments that align with an end-of-year summative assessment (either state, district, or teacher created); and <br><br> Anticipates student reaction to content; allocation of time per unit is flexible and/or reflects level of difficulty of each unit. |
| **Effective (Level 3)** | Based on achievement goals, teacher plans units by: <br><br> Identifying content standards that students will master in each unit; <br><br> Creating assessments before each unit begins for backwards planning; and <br><br> Allocating an instructionally appropriate amount of time for each unit. |

| | |
|---|---|
| **Improvement Necessary (Level 2)** | Based on achievement goals, teacher plans units by:<br><br>Identifying content standards that students will master in each unit.<br><br>Teacher may not:<br><br>Create assessments before each unit begins for backwards planning; and/or<br><br>Allocate an instructionally appropriate amount of time for each unit. |
| **Ineffective (Level 1)** | Teacher rarely or never plans units by identifying content standards that students will master in each unit and/or there is little to no evidence that teacher plans units at all. |
| **Indicator 4e** | The teacher tracks student data and analyzes progress throughout the course of the school year. |
| **Highly Effective (Level 4)** | A teacher fulfills the criteria for Effective and additionally:<br><br>Uses daily checks for understanding for additional data points;<br><br>Updates tracking system regularly; and<br><br>Uses data analysis of student progress to drive lesson planning for the following day. |
| **Effective (Level 3)** | Teacher uses an effective data tracking system for:<br><br>Recording student assessment/progress data;<br><br>Analyzing student progress toward mastery and planning future lessons/units accordingly; and<br><br>Maintaining a grading system aligned to student learning goals. |
| **Improvement Necessary (Level 2)** | Teacher uses an effective data tracking system for:<br><br>Recording student assessment/progress data; and<br><br>Maintaining a grading system.<br><br>Teacher may not:<br><br>Use data to analyze student progress toward mastery or to plan future lessons/units; and/or<br><br>Have a grading system that appropriately aligns with student learning goals. |
| **Ineffective (Level 1)** | Teacher rarely or never uses a data tracking system to record student assessment/progress data and/or has no discernable grading system. |

## B2: SDH (Secondary department head) Roles

 **SECONDARY DEPARTMENT HEAD**

### *Responsibilities:*
- Evaluation and supervision of teaching staff
- Development of curriculum
- Alignment of assessments
- Development of instructional practices
- Management of Professional Learning Communities
- Department "voice"
- Provide support for curriculum implementation
- Provide professional development opportunities for the department
- H.S. Department management (i.e., ordering, textbooks)
- Communication with M.S. Department chairs
- Hiring of new staff
- Facilitation of textbook adoption

### *Possibilities:*
- Modeling and coaching of PLC processes
- Co-teaching
- Class coverage for learning walk opportunities
- Mentor
- Resource for classroom management strategies, parent communication assistance, instructional practices, and technology

# B3: Book Resources for PLC Implementation

## Prior to Implementation

- *Cultures Built to Last: Systemic PLCs at Work* by Richard DuFour and Michael Fullan

- *Leaders of Learning: How District, School, and Classroom Leaders Improve Student Achievement* by Richard DuFour and Robert J. Marzano

- *Working Inside the Black Box: Assessment for Learning in the Classroom* by Paul Black, Christine Harrison, Clare Lee, Bethan Marshall, and Dylan Williams

- *Learning by Doing: A Handbook for Professional Learning Communities at Work* by Richard DuFour, Rebecca DuFour, Robert Eaker, and Thomas Many

- *Professional Learning Communities at Work: Best Practices for Enhancing Student Achievement* by Richard DuFour and Robert Eaker

## Continuation of Our PLC Studies

- *Groups at Work: Strategies and Structures for Professional Learning* by Laura Lipton and Bruce Wellman

- *Leading Groups: Effective Strategies for Building Professional Community* by Laura Lipton and Bruce Wellman

- *Focus: Elevating the Essentials to Radically Improve Student Learning* by Mike Schmoker

- *The Five Disciplines of PLC Leaders* by Timothy D. Kanold

- *Facilitating Teacher Teams and Authentic PLCs: The Human Side of Leading People, Protocols, and Practices* by Daniel R. Venables

- *Turning the Flywheel: A Monograph to Accompany* Good to Great by Jim Collins

# B4: PLC Agenda Example

BROWNSBURG COMMUNITY SCHOOL CORPORATION
SECONDARY SCIENCE PLC AGENDA & NOTES

DATE:                                          PLC:

| PLC/PGP GOAL | Building Goals |
|---|---|
|  |  |

**PLC Reflective Questions to Ponder/Guide You**

- What is a data strategy that will lead us to dig deeper into our data?
- How do we authentically reflect on our PLC process and student learning?
- How can you more closely tie your PGP "action research" to your weekly PLC process?
- How do we foster growth amongst each other and students through student-centered reflections/discussions in our PLC meetings?

**Celebrations**

**What Do We Want Students to Know?**

**How Do We Know That Students Have Mastered the Objective(s)?**

**What Will We Do With the Students Based Off Their Current Level of Mastery (Re-teach/Enrichment)?**

**How Will What You Did in PLC Today Impact Students?**

**Tasks for Next Time:**

# B5: PLC Leadership Summit Example

**Brownsburg Community School Corporation**
**6th Annual Leadership Summit**
**Brownsburg East Middle School**

| | |
|---|---|
| 8:00 a.m. | Welcome and Introductions |
| 8:05 a.m. | Lesson Design and PLC: How do they fit? Successful PLC: Connecting Prior Learning |
| 9:15 a.m. | Breakout Sessions (Select from one session listed below) |
| 10:15 a.m. | Breakout Sessions (Select from one session listed below) |
| 11:00 a.m. | Lunch |
| Noon | School Team Time (Teams can meet at BEMS or their schools) |

**Sessions** (All sessions are offered two times):

**Title:** *PLC 101: Tools for Being an Effective PLC Leader*
**Audience:** PLC leaders in their first or second year of leading PLC
**Room Assignment:** F124
**Session Summary:** This session will focus on the primary elements of successful PLCS.

**Title:** *PLC 201: Developing Additional Skills as a PLC Leader* (Elementary)
**Audience:** Experienced elementary PLC leaders
**Room Assignment:** F125
**Session Summary:** This session will focus on taking our PLCs to the next level. Participants will explore what is already making a strong system of PLCs in BCSC. They will then discover what may be done to make their meetings and work with team members exceptional.

**Title:** *PLC 201: Developing Additional Skills as a PLC Leader* (Secondary)
**Audience:** Experienced secondary PLC leaders
**Room Assignment:** F126
**Session Summary:** PLC leaders will walk away with a greater understanding of what makes a GREAT PLC and what actions steps are necessary to lead their groups to be truly GREAT.

**Title:** *The Top 3 Challenges of Leading a Successful PLC* (Elementary)
**Audience:** Elementary PLC leaders
**Room Assignment:** G101
**Session Summary:** Even the best PLCs have their roadblocks and setbacks at times! As leaders, it is our job to minimize them and keep moving ahead. This session will focus on the barriers and "in-flight" strategies that PLC leaders can expect and utilize during their weekly PLC meetings. Scenarios will be demonstrated by team members followed by small-group discussion and strategies to take to your first PLC.

**Title:** *The Top 3 Challenges of Leading a Successful PLC* (Secondary)
**Audience:** Secondary PLC leaders
**Room Assignment:** LGI
**Session Summary:** If you could "fix" anything in your PLC meetings, what would it be? In this session, we will share the top obstacles faced by PLC leaders and you will leave with solutions that you can use immediately for these obstacles! A real PLC simulation, group discussion, and time to develop individual PLC growth goals and receive feedback from other leaders will be a part of this session.

# B6: PGP Think Sheet

## PGP Faculty Meeting Think Sheet

With your PLC:

1. What is your current ISTEP pass rate? _____
2. What gaps exist in your data?
   a. Special Education _____
   b. Free/Reduced _____
   c. Non-White _____
   d. ENL _____
3. Which gap do you need to address? _____
4. If there is no gap, please focus on the goal of increasing ISTEP scores.
5. Write your goal in TalentEd.

Examples:

1. As a PLC, we will strive to hold 97% of our students at core and save 45% of students from DNP to Pass on the 2018 ISTEP Test. In my classroom currently, _____% of my students are passing the _____ portion of the 2017 ISTEP. In order to save 45% of DNP, I will need to focus on _____ number of students on my roster. Holding 97% of students at core and adding the number of students listed above, my pass rate for my classroom on the 2018 ISTEP test will be _____%. Additionally, there is a gap of _____% between _____ & _____ on this portion of the test. Through intentional lesson design and PLCs, that gap will be cut by a third to _____ % on the 2018 ISTEP test.

2. Currently, _____% of my students are at Pass+ on the _____ portion of the 2016 ISTEP. Through focused enrichment/extension of learning, my Pass+ rate for the _____ portion of the 2017 ISTEP test will be _____%.

3. My goal for the 2017–18 school year will be for _____ % to reach mastery on the _____ end-of-year common assessment. Additionally, there is currently a gap of _____% between _____ & _____ on my roster. Through intentional lesson design and PLCs, that gap will be cut by a third _____% on this assessment.

With your PLC:

1. Discuss the gaps found in your data.
2. What are some action steps your PLC might need to take to make your goals a reality?
3. How will you monitor your individual progress and your PLCs progress toward reaching that goal?

## B7: PGP Timeline and Steps

### PGP Goals
#### Timelines/Alignment

- *PGP Goal Submission* (by Labor Day)
  - PGP Think Sheet is utilized
  - PLC members work together to create a similar SMART goal, that aligns with their School Building Goals (which in turn align with the District Goals).

- *PGP Goal Review #1* (Before Thanksgiving)
  - Summarize what you have done up to this check-in point to reach your PGP goal. How has your data changed since the beginning of the year? (Attach data to PGP)
  - What is the data telling you? What can you infer? What are action steps that you will take to move closer to your PGP goal?
  - What other pieces of information would you like to share with your administrator? What supports do you need?

- *PGP Goal Review #2* (Before Spring Break)
  - Same reflective questions as in Goal Review #1

- *PGP Goal Final Submission* (End of School Year)
  - End of Year Summary
    » Using student data, share the status of your SMART Goal. Be sure to specifically state how student learning was impacted (Attach final data).
    » What successes and/or lessons learned do you have to share?
    » How has this experience impacted future goal setting efforts? (If SMART Goal is continued to the following school year, describe what strategies will be utilized to increase student learning.)
    » Additional supports needed?

## B8: PGP Goal Cycle

## Brownsburg School Corporation Goal Cycle

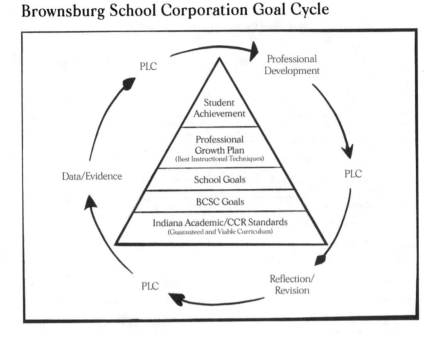

The basis of all goals must begin with state or common core standards for education. Beyond that, corporations should create clear and minimal district goals that feed to school goals. From the school level, PLCs should create their focus that each individual teacher then contributes to. Clarity in goals leads to higher student achievement.

# C1: Hiring Process Protocol

**Brownsburg Community School Corporation**
**SECONDARY Teacher Hiring Process**

| Departments with Secondary Department Heads (SDHs) | Other Secondary Departments (Fine Arts, etc.) |
|---|---|
| ☐ Principal notifies SDH and HR of open position and reason for the opening (replacing someone, new, temporary contract, etc.) | ☐ Principal notifies HR of open position and reason for the opening (replacing someone, new, temporary contract, etc.) |
| ☐ HR posts the position, if necessary (positions typically posted for 5 business days) | ☐ HR posts the position, if necessary (positions typically posted for 5 business days) |
| ☐ SDH is notified of recommended candidates to be included in the interview process by the application deadline, if any | ☐ Principal is notified of recommended candidates to be included in the interview process, if any |
| ☐ SDH reviews candidate materials, selects candidates for initial interviews, checking that the license, HQ status, and other credentials are acceptable | ☐ Principal and HR review candidate materials, select candidates for initial interviews, checking that the license, HQ status, and other credentials are acceptable |
| ☐ SDH schedules and conducts initial interviews with interview team | ☐ Principal schedules and conducts initial interviews with interview team |
| ☐ SDH notes in Applitrack those selected for an initial interview | ☐ Principal notes in Applitrack those selected for an initial interview |
| ☐ SDH schedules and conducts model lesson interview with Principal and Assistant Superintendent (and Director of Special Education, if applicable); if temporary contract position, a model lesson may not be required | ☐ Principal schedules and conducts model lesson interview with Principal and Assistant Superintendent (and Director of Special Education, if applicable); if temporary contract position, a model lesson may not be required |
| ☐ SDH notifies candidates not selected for model lesson interview | ☐ Principal notifies candidates not selected for model lesson interview |
| ☐ SDH notes in Applitrack model lesson information | ☐ Principal notes in Applitrack model lesson information |
| ☐ SDH checks references on selected candidate | ☐ Principal checks references on selected candidate |
| ☐ Principal contacts selected candidate | ☐ Principal contacts selected candidate |
| ☐ Principal notifies HR of selected candidate and teaching assignment of the candidate; HR verifies candidate credentials | ☐ Principal notifies HR of selected candidate and teaching assignment of the candidate; HR verifies candidate credentials |
| ☐ Principal schedules candidate meeting with Superintendent (temporary contract candidates do NOT have to meet with the Superintendent) **PLEASE NOTE,** a copy of the application packet AND the completed reference check form must be submitted to HR <u>prior to</u> the candidate meeting with the Superintendent | ☐ Principal schedules candidate meeting with Superintendent (temporary contract candidates do NOT have to meet with the Superintendent) **PLEASE NOTE,** a copy of the application packet AND the completed reference check form must be submitted to HR <u>prior to</u> the candidate meeting with the Superintendent |
| ☐ Superintendent shares results of candidate meeting with Principal and HR, including specifics of employment offer; Principal shares results with SDH | ☐ Superintendent shares results of candidate meeting with Principal and HR, including specifics of employment offer |
| ☐ SDH contacts selected candidate (<u>HS:</u> SDH conducts tour, shares building-level introductory training, activities, etc.; <u>MS:</u> SDH instructs candidate to contact building principal to schedule tour and get building-level information) | ☐ Principal contacts selected candidate (includes sharing building-level introductory training, activities, etc.) |
| ☐ SDH communicates with HR to send new-hire information | ☐ Principal communicates with HR to send new-hire information |
| ☐ HR contacts candidate regarding background check, employment paperwork, and any materials still needed (transcripts, etc.) | ☐ HR contacts candidate regarding background check, employment paperwork, and any materials still needed (transcripts, etc.) |
| ☐ SDH notifies other considered candidates not selected and completes remaining notes in Applitrack; HR notifies the other candidates not selected in the full "pool" of candidates | ☐ Principal notifies other candidates not selected and completes remaining notes in Applitrack |
| ☐ HR submits candidate name to the Board for approval once background check is complete and forwards information to technology for account creation | ☐ HR submits candidate name to the Board for approval once background check is complete and forwards information to technology for account creation |

# C2: Sample Model Lesson Document

## Brownsburg Community School Corporation
### Secondary Science Teacher – Model Lesson

The next step of the interview process will include delivering a model lesson to the secondary science administrator and the assistant superintendent.

The model lesson will take place at Central Office. The room will be equipped with an easel, a dry erase board, wireless internet connection, computer, projector, and screen. Note: You will need to access your documents through your email or the internet (not via a flash drive).

Please plan materials and bring two copies of the lesson plan. For the purposes of the model lesson, the interview team will act as your students.

The lesson should:

1. focus on the following Indiana Academic Science Standard: /C.4.5—stoichiometry specifically limiting reactants/. Include information on the lessons leading up to this lesson and the lessons to follow;
2. be interactive, student-centered, and engaging for secondary students;
3. demonstrate your understanding for educational rigor and relevance;
4. demonstrate methods of differentiation; and
5. incorporate checks for understanding.

You will have no more than three minutes to set up "your class" prior to teaching the lesson. You will be asked to briefly explain your lesson and then teach the **most engaging 12–15 minutes** of the lesson. Following the teaching segment, the interview team may ask follow-up questions.

The model lesson will be followed by a question-and-answer segment. The total time for the model lesson and the question-and-answer segment will be 30 minutes.

The interview team will be assessing:

- Quality and organization of the lesson
- Age appropriateness of the lesson
- Professionalism during the teaching segment and the question-and-answer segment
- Depth of understanding of best practice demonstrated in the development of the lesson and during the question-and-answer segment

This is your opportunity to give us a snapshot of what the children of the Brownsburg Community School Corporation would experience in your classroom on a daily basis.

If you have any questions or have additional technology needs beyond those listed above, please contact (insert contact).

# D1: DOK (Depth of Knowledge) Resource

## A Guide to Focused Questioning

| Are you focused on *what* you are asking your students and *how* you are assessing understanding through your verbal and written questions?<br><br>**FOCUS ON THE *HOW* AND *WHY* TO DIVE DEEP INTO LEARNING.** | | | | | |
|---|---|---|---|---|---|
| | | **Subjects and example questions for each DOK level** | | | |
| **Webb's Depth of Knowledge** | **Question Type** (key DOK words underlined) | **Language Arts** | **Math** | **Science** | **Social Studies** |
| **DOK LEVEL 1** (Basic Recall)<br><br>*Time spent at DOK Level 1 should be minimal.* | <u>Recalling</u> key plot events<br><br><u>Defining</u> words or concepts<br><br><u>Measuring</u> or calculating distances or solutions<br><br><u>Identifying</u> concepts | Who is the main character in Chapter 1?<br><br>What is the definition of *theme?*<br><br>Label the parts of the plot diagram for the short story.<br><br>Recite the prologue from *Romeo and Juliet.* | What is the first step that should be used in order to isolate the variable and maintain a balanced equation for the following? $7x + 9 = 23$<br><br>Two angles of an obtuse triangle are 35 degrees and 45 degrees. Calculate the measure of the third angle. | Which cell organelle is responsible for building proteins?<br><br>Which type of rock is formed under great pressure and high temperatures?<br><br>Using information form the Periodic Table, how many protons does one atom of Carbon have? | Define compromise.<br><br>Identify two examples of political conflict among individuals and/ or groups in the United States during the colonial time period.<br><br>List three physical characteristics of a region of the United States. |

Are you focused on *what* you are asking your students and *how* you are assessing understanding through your verbal and written questions?

**FOCUS ON THE *HOW* AND *WHY* TO DIVE DEEP INTO LEARNING.**

| | | Subjects and example questions for each DOK level | | | |
|---|---|---|---|---|---|
| Webb's Depth of Knowledge | Question Type (key DOK words underlined) | Language Arts | Math | Science | Social Studies |
| **DOK LEVEL 2** (Skill/Concept) *Ensure that DOK Level 2 skills are present in students and that concepts are solid in order to move deeper.* | Demonstrating cause and effect Predicting events or outcomes Making inferences Distinguishing differences between subjects/things Relating content to other ideas or life | What causes the character to flee and what is the effect of her departure from her family? What do you think might happen next in the story? What might be the cause of the character's stress? | If you were asked to find the amount of paint needed to paint walls, floor, and ceiling of a game room, would you need to calculate volume or surface area? Explain your thinking. One angle of a triangle has a measure of 30 degrees. What are the possibilities for the other two angles? How will your answers change if you are told that the triangle must be an acute triangle? | (Given a food web) Which organisms would be considered primary or first order consumers and why? Create a multi-flow (cause and effect) Thinking Map showing the relationship between deforestation and the environment. Create a line graph depicting a person driving a car. Make sure to label the axes and include what the graph would look like when the person hits the gas, brakes, and stops. | Why did most colonial farmers settle near oceans or coastal waterways? Explain the reasons why discrimination developed in the United States prior to the civil rights movement. Explain the causes and effects of the Revolutionary War. What was the most significant economic impact of the transcontinental railroads during the late 1800s? |

Are you focused on *what* you are asking your students and *how* you are assessing understanding through your verbal and written questions?

**FOCUS ON THE *HOW* AND *WHY* TO DIVE DEEP INTO LEARNING.**

| Webb's Depth of Knowledge | Question Type (key DOK words underlined) | Subjects and example questions for each DOK level | | | |
| --- | --- | --- | --- | --- | --- |
| | | Language Arts | Math | Science | Social Studies |
| **DOK LEVEL 3** (Strategic Thinking) <br><br> *Your questions for discussion, classwork, and test questions should target this deeper level DOK.* | Assessing the effect or purpose <br><br> Drawing conclusions to hypothesize a possible outcome <br><br> Revising to show improvement <br><br> Using concepts to solve a problem or pose a solution <br><br> Citing evidence to support an idea | What is the purpose of the dark colors of the character's clothing? <br><br> How does the author's voice change in this chapter? <br><br> Use supporting evidence to prove the novel's main theme. <br><br> Determine the author's purpose and describe how it affects your interpretation of reading the speech. | Smallville Middle School has set a goal to raise money for the Toys for Tots program. The sixth grade has 200 students and raised $1,400. The seventh grade has 250 students and raised $1,250. The eighth grade has 225 students and raised $1,800. Which of the following statements is not true? Justify your answer in words and with a diagram. <br><br> The eighth grade raised the most money per student. <br><br> If the sixth grade had raised $200 more, their amount per student would be the same as the amount per eighth grade student. | Compare a distance vs. time graph with an acceleration vs. time graph for the same moving object. Explain your findings. <br><br> Read three scholarly articles about water pollution and write an essay discussing your findings and explaining how you can personally reduce water pollution in your home or school. | Recognize and explain misconceptions related to the discovery of America. <br><br> Justify the Democratic and/or Republican party platforms expressed in a series of debates. <br><br> Using examples to justify your answer, explain the powers of government established by the Preamble to the United States Constitution and why these powers are still significant today. |

Are you focused on *what* you are asking your students and *how* you are assessing understanding through your verbal and written questions?

## FOCUS ON THE *HOW* AND *WHY* TO DIVE DEEP INTO LEARNING.

| | | Subjects and example questions for each DOK level | | | |
|---|---|---|---|---|---|
| Webb's Depth of Knowledge | Question Type (key DOK words underlined) | Language Arts | Math | Science | Social Studies |
| DOK LEVEL 4 (Extended Thinking) <br><br> *\* DOK Level 4 questions usually require multiple steps and usually integrate multiple concepts.* | <u>Creating</u> a product <br><br> <u>Proving</u> an idea or hypothesis <br><br> <u>Synthesizing</u> multiple understanding <br><br> <u>Connecting</u> concepts to relevant ideas <br><br> <u>Critiquing</u> concepts to discuss strengths, weakness, effect, etc. <br><br> <u>Designing</u> a product | Describe and illustrate how the theme from this unit is found in multiple texts. <br><br> Create a research paper to analyze the important role family history plays in an author's fiction writing. <br><br> Synthesize multiple texts from the unit to analyze universal themes found throughout each work. | TASK: You plan to sell 300 ice cream cones at a sports event. You buy ice cream in 1-liter tubs at $2 each. Each cone sells for 5 cents, and you plan to sell each filled cone for 80 cents. <br><br> Before buying the ice cream, you survey 60 people and find out the follow-ing preferences: MINT-10%, STRAW-BERRY-25%, CHOC CHIP-15%, VANILLA-50%. <br><br> Work out the quantities you need to buy and calculate those costs. Show how much profit you expect to make on that day. Show all work and give a written justification for your answers. | Design and conduct a science investigation that involves collecting, organizing, and interpreting data as well as effectively communicating your findings. <br><br> Research a local ecological problem and work with a team to develop a practical solution. Implement the solution if possible. | Propose solutions for today's economic crisis. Predict outcomes for each solution. <br><br> Create your own party and party platform. Include three to five issues and be prepared to present and debate those issues. |

## D2: Formative Assessment Example

**Considerations to make when creating formative assessments:**

1. Check the understanding of *all* students.
2. Assess during the lesson whenever possible.
3. Keep formatives short and focused.
4. Assess one skill or standard when possible.
5. Provide timely, actionable feedback to students.

**Quick Check:**

Who was the conqueror who took over ancient Greece?

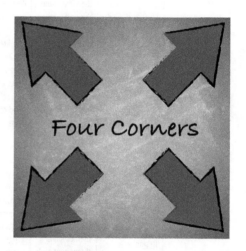

1. Dionysus
2. Alexander the Great
3. Socrates
4. Pericles

This question was designed for a mid-lesson check for understanding. The question was posted for the students, who were then to move to the corner of the room that the teacher designated for that letter choice.

# D3: Common Summative Assessment Format

**Considerations to make when creating formative assessments:**

1. Questions on the assessment must match the depth of knowledge of the standards being assessed

2. Formatting, especially spacing and white space, makes an impact on the accessibility of the exam for all students.

3. Variety types of questions should align with the state or national benchmark examples (i.e., True/False questions should not appear on your summative).

4. Organize by topic or standard to provide clarity of focus for students.

Example on next page.

**Earth Science Summative Assessment (45 points)**

**Multiple Choice:** Identify the choice that best completes the statement or answers the question. Place the answer in the correct location on your answer sheet.

**(8.ESS.2)**

1.  The ___ energy creates convection cycles in our atmosphere.
    a. Sun's          c. Moon's
    b. Water cycle's  d. Earth's

2.  Which process of the water cycle is affected by the Sun's energy?
    a. runoff          c. evaporation
    b. infiltration    d. none of the above

3.  Gravity has an impact on the water cycle. Which statements are correct examples of this?
    I.   Gravity pulls water vapor up to the clouds.
    II.  Gravity pulls water down into the ground.
    III. Gravity pushes up, then pulls down water.
    IV.  Gravity pulls water back down to Earth.
        a. I and II        c. II and IV
        b. I and III       d. I, II and III

4.  The Sun's energy drives the water cycle. Which statement is correct?
    a. The sun heats groundwater and changes it to a gas.
    b. The sun heats water vapor, causing it to condense into a cloud.
    c. The sun chases the water into the ground, causing it to infiltrate.
    d. The sun heats the surface water, causing it to turn to a gas.

5.  Water that is not evaporated or does not flow into a body of water but absorbs into the ground. This is an example of _____.
    a. condensation    c. evaporation
    b. runoff          d. infiltration

6.  Water vapor released by plants is _____.
    a. evaporation     c. infiltration
    b. transpiration   d. Condensation

# E1: PLC Norms

## Developing Norms Worksheet

| When Establishing Norms, Consider | Proposed Norm |
|---|---|
| **Listening**<br><br>• How will we encourage listening?<br><br>• How will we discourage interrupting? | |
| **Preparation**<br><br>• What are the expectations for being prepared for an upcoming PLC meeting?<br><br>• How do we ensure everyone is prepared to address all agenda items? | |
| **Participation and Decision-Making**<br><br>• How do we increase our shared leadership?<br><br>• How will we encourage everyone's participation?<br><br>• How will we make decisions?<br><br>• How will we deal with conflicts? | |
| **Efficiency and Productivity**<br><br>• What norms are needed to ensure we are making the most of our time together?<br><br>• Who/how will we monitor and redirect when we aren't? | |
| **Data Norms**<br><br>• How will we monitor our data?<br><br>• What type of data are we bringing? In what ways are we analyzing the data?<br><br>• How will we push ourselves in the area of data? | |

| When Establishing Norms, Consider | Proposed Norm |
|---|---|
| **Reflective Process**<br><br>• How can we ensure our group is reflective throughout the PLC process?<br>• How do we bring focus and accountability to the reflective process?<br>• How will we wrap around to the previous PLC? | |
| **PLC Goals/SMART Goals** | |

## F1: PLC Framework

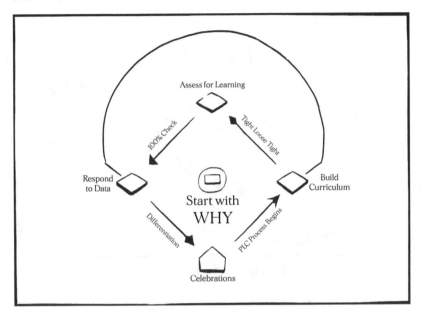

## The four guiding questions for all PLCs:

1. What do we want our students to know?
2. How will we know they've learned it?
3. What we will do for students who don't understand?
4. How will we enrich students who do understand?

## G1: Intervention J Curve

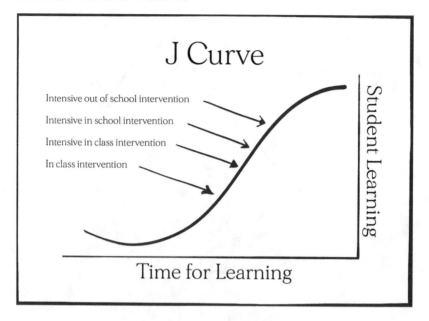

J Curve is a belief that given more time and intervention, students can find success in learning.

# Index

# References

Abrams, J. (2016). *Hard conversations unpacked*. Thousand Oaks, CA: Corwin..

Ainsworth, L. (2003). *"Unwrapping" the standards: A simple process to make standards manageable*. Englewood, CO: Advance Learning Press.

Bergeson, T *(2006)*. *Race, poverty, and academic achievement*. Available on http://www.doh.wa.gov/SBOH/ESS/documents/Race&Poverty.pdf

Bloomberg, P., & Pitchford, B. (2016). *Leading impact teams: Building a culture of efficacy*. Thousand Oaks, CA: Corwin.

Brookhart, S., & Moss, M. (2009). *Advancing formative assessment in every classroom: A guide for instructional leaders*. Alexandria, VA: ASCD.

Cobb, F., & Krownapple, J. (2019). *Belonging through a culture of dignity*. Mimi-Todd Press.

Collins, J. (2001). *Good to great*. New York, NY: Harper Business.

Davies, Anne (2011). *Making Classroom Assessment Work*. Solution Tree, 3rd edition.

De Bono, Edward (1999). *Six Thinking Hats: An Essential Approach to Business Management*. Boston, MA: Little, Brown and Company.

DuFour, R., & Marzano, R. (2011). *Leaders of learning*. Bloomington, IN: Solutions Tree Press.

DuFour, R., DuFour, R., Eaker, R., & Many, T. (2006). *Learning by doing: A handbook for professional learning communities at work*. Bloomington, IN: Solutions Tree Press.

DuFour, R., & Fullan, M. (2013) *Cultures built to last: Systemic PLCs at work.* Bloomington, IN: Solutions Tree Press.

Fisher, D., & Frey, N. (2007). *Checking for understanding.* Alexandria, VA: ASCD.

Hall, G. E., & Hord, S. M. (2006). *Implementing change: Patterns, principles, and potholes.* Livonia, MI: Pearson/Allyn & Bacon.

Hattie, J. (2012). *Visible learning for teachers.* New York, NY: Routledge.

Kanold, T. D. (2011). *The five disciplines of PLC leaders.* Bloomington, IN: Solutions Tree Press.

Knight, J. (2007). *Instructional coaching.* Thousand Oaks, CA: Corwin.

Lemov, D. (2010). *Teach like a champion.* San Francisco, CA: Jossey-Bass.

Lemov, D. (2015). *Teach like a champion 2.0: 62 techniques that put students on the path to college.* San Francisco, CA: Jossey-Bass.

Lipton, L., & Wellman, B. (2011). *Groups at work: Strategies and structures for professional learning.* Sherman, CT: MiraVia, LLC.

Marzano, R. J., Pickering, D. J., & Pollock, J. E. (2001). *Classroom instruction that works.* Alexandria, VA: ASCD.

Marzano, R., & Waters, T. (2009). *District leadership that works.* Bloomington, IN: Solution Tree.

Pfeffer, P., & Sutton, R. (2000). *The knowing–doing gap.* Boston, MA: Harvard Business School Press.

Schmoker, M. (2018). *Focus.* Alexandria, VA: ASCD.

Schmoker, M. (2016). *Leading with focus.* Alexandria, VA: ASCD.

Sinek, S. (2009). *Start with the why.* New York, NY: Penguin.

Stiggins, R. (1994). *Student-centered classroom assessment.* New York, NY: Merrill.

Venables, D. (2018). *Facilitating teacher teams and authentic PLCs.* Alexandria, VA: ASCD.

Waterman, R. (1987). *The Renewal Factor: How the Best Get and Keep the Competitive Edge.* Bantam.

Wiggins, G., & McTighe, J. (2005). *Understanding by design.* Alexandria, VA: ASCD.

# About the Authors

CARRIE ROSEBROCK is a Professional Learning Specialist for the Central Indiana Educational Service Center in Indianapolis, Indiana. She teaches and presents at schools and centers across the state. Before joining the CIESC team, she served as the Secondary English Administrator for Brownsburg Community School Corporation. She works with schools to improve their PLC processes, instructional leadership, curriculum and assessment development and teacher leadership.

Carrie earned her undergraduate degree in Secondary English Education from Indiana University, and earned her Masters in School Administration from Butler University. She currently lives in Brownsburg, Indiana, with her husband Brad, and their two children, Grace and Will.

You can find more resources from Carrie by visiting carrierosebrock.com or connecting with her on social media at @CarrieRosebrock

SARAH HENRY is the Secondary Science Administrator for Brownsburg Community School Corporation where she works with secondary science teachers to improve curriculum, instruction, assessment, and PLC processes. She has presented workshops at the local, state, and national level as well as educational consulting for districts around the  state. She has taught aspiring educational leaders, as an adjunct professor, in the area of Assessing for Learning for several years.

Sarah earned her undergraduate degree in Elementary Education with a Secondary endorsement in Science from Butler University, and earned her Masters degree in Educational Leadership from the University of Indianapolis. She currently lives in Brownsburg, Indiana, with her husband Erik, and their two children, Jenna and Brennan.

You can find more resources from Sarah by visiting SarahDHenry.com or connecting with her on social media at @MrsSarahHenry; @Sarah_D_Henry

CPSIA information can be obtained
at www.ICGtesting.com
Printed in the USA
LVHW080444161021
700568LV00024B/323